Sammy Cahn's Rhyming Dictionary

ISBN   0-89724-633-0

Sammy Cahn's Rhyming Dictionary

Acknowledgments

For permission to reproduce song lyrics, acknowledgment is gratefully made to the following:

Lyrics from the following songs are reproduced from SONGS WITH LYRICS by Sammy Cahn, Cahn Music Co. 9000 Sunset Blvd., Penthouse, Los Angeles, CA 90069-1819. "The Second Time Around"; "The Tender Trap"; "Call Me Irresponsible"; "Let It Snow!"; "You're My Girl"; "It's Magic"; "The Christmas Waltz"; "I'll Walk Alone"; "It's Been a Long, Long Time"; "I Fall in Love Too Easily"; "Saturday Night Is the Loneliest Night of the Week."

"I've Grown Accustomed to Her Face." Alan J. Lerner and Frederick Lowe. Copyright © 1956 by Alan J. Lerner and Frederick Lowe. Chappell & Co., Inc., owner of publication and allied rights throughout the world. International Copyright Secured. All Rights Reserved.

"Jingle, Jangle, Jingle (I've Got Spurs...)." Words by Frank Loesser/Music by Joseph J. Lilley. Copyright © 1942 by Paramount Music Corporation. Copyright Renewed 1969 by Paramount Music Corporation.

"The Darktown Strutters Ball." by Shelton Brooks. © 1917 Leo Feist, Inc. © Renewal 1945 Leo Feist, Inc. All Rights Assigned to CBS SONGS, a Division of CBS INC. International Copyright Secured. All Rights Reserved.

"How Deep Is the Ocean?" by Irving Berlin. Published by Irving Berlin Music Corporation. Copyright © 1932 Irving Berlin. Copyright renewed 1959 by Irving Berlin.

"Oh, What a Beautiful Morning." Richard Rodgers and Oscar Hammerstein. © 1943 by Williamson Music Co. Copyright Renewed. International Copyright Secured. All Rights Reserved.

"Carolina in the Morning." by Gus Kahn and Walter Donaldson. Copyright 1922 Gilbert Keyes Music Company. (Pursuant to Sections 304(c) and 401(b) of the U.S. Copyright Law.)

"High Hopes." Words by Sammy Cahn/Music by James Van Heusen. Copyright © 1959 Sincap Productions. Copyright © 1959 Maraville Music Corporation.

"Come Fly with Me." Words by Sammy Cahn/Music by James Van Heusen. Copyright © 1958 Maraville Music Corporation.

"I Only Have Eyes for You." Lyric by Al Dubin/Music by Harry Warren. © 1934 (Renewed) Warner Bros. Inc. All Rights Reserved.

"Thoroughly Modern Millie." Words by Sammy Cahn/Music by James Van Heusen. © Copyright 1967 by Northern Music Company, New York, N.Y. Rights Administered by MCA Music, A Division of MCA Inc., New York, N.Y. All Rights Reserved.

For Tita, Steve, Laurie, Heath and Rachel
with copywritten love!!!
Special Thanks to Frank Military and Jay Morgenstern

Pronunciation Key

Vowels

ā	cave	ī	mine	oi	boys
ä	father	ĭ	tip	ou	how
ă	tab	ō	mow	o͞o	you
ē	bee	ô	raw	ŭ	tuck
ĕ	let	o͝o	good	ə	around, brother, edible, wallop, consensus

Consonants

b	big	l	lamp	th	think
ch	church	m	man	th	father
d	dead	n	nod	v	valet
f	fake	p	pod	w	wallet
g	good	r	rod	y	you
h	hood	s	salt	z	crazy
j	jelly	sh	fashion	zh	decision
k	king	t	top		

Contents

o

u

Introduction

I am often asked, Which comes first—the words or the music? I answer that what comes first is the phone call asking you to write a song.

I am also asked, What is the difference between a poem and a lyric? My answer is that a poem is meant for the eye, while a lyric is meant for the ear, but both reach the mind and touch the heart. Shakespeare, though he was a master poet, would have made a poor lyrist.* Just try to sing "Love can laugh at locksmiths." If the word *orange* is unrhymable, *locksmiths* is unsingable. And singability is the difference between a poem and a lyric.

Once I have written a song and have considered all of the pros and cons of the lyric, the uppermost and final consideration is, Does it sing? and not only sing, but sing effortlessly. The cadences of the lyric must leave the most subtle breathing spaces, as must the music. Words will not sing unless they are properly wedded to the proper notes. For this reason, no matter which composer I've worked with, when a song is finished, we spend just as many if not more hours over the demonstration of the song as we did writing it. (I have even been called a "lethal song demonstrator" because I put across the story line of the song by *lean-ing into it* and *e-nun-ci-a-ting* every word.)

I believe anyone can learn the concept of singability and that anyone can write lyrics. All you need are the rhyming words and something to say. As a youngster I learned how to write a song by playing a game. I would take the words from other great lyrists of the day and change them. (I still do this today, although now I get paid for it!) But perhaps the best way to emphasize the importance of singability is by relating how, and why, I wrote some of my songs.

---

* *Lyricist* may be more commonly used than *lyrist*, but I prefer *lyrist* and will use it throughout.

I'll start by telling you about my first meeting with Bing Crosby and about the score that the talented Jimmy Van Heusen and I wrote for a new film Crosby would be starring in.

Van Heusen was an old hand at this since he had worked on so many films with Johnny Burke, Bing's favorite lyrist, and the man who gave me my first rhyming dictionary. Van Heusen and I went to Bing's home on Mapleton Drive in Holmby Hills, and I didn't just sing our song to Bing, I *really* sang that song. When I finished, Bing looked at me and said, "You're pretty good."

"Pretty good?" I said, "I'm the best."

I was extremely pleased that Bing liked our song and even more pleased that he was placing me in the same league as Mack Gordon.* What was the name of our song and how did it come to be? I'll explain.

I was delighted at having the chance to work with Bing. However, my joyous anticipation was shattered when I read the script. Crosby was supposed to play a widower who had achieved everything in life except a college degree. In the space of two reels he decides to go back to school, meets an attractive widow, his French teacher, and they fall in love. Ask yourself what sort of a ballad do you write for a widow and a widower?

Van Heusen and I swiftly eliminated titles like "You Could Be the Death of Me" and one or two others equally macabre. Then one day I turned to Van Heusen and said, "Do you like the title 'The Second Time Around?'"

Van Heusen asked, "How do you mean, 'the title'?"

I replied, " 'Love is wonderful, the second time around, just as beautiful, with both feet on the ground. . . .'"

Van Heusen said, "You mean 'Love is lovelier, the second time around, just as wonderful, with both feet on the ground. . . .'"

I agreed, of course. When I am writing a song, I write in a fury and then "neaten up" the lyrics later on.

We began:

> Love is lovelier
> The second time around,
> Just as wonderful
> With both feet on the ground.

---

* Mack Gordon, legendary lyrist and song demonstrator, writer of "You'll Never Know," "Chatanooga Choo-Choo," "You Make Me Feel So Young," and many more.

> It's that second time you hear your love song sung,
> Makes you think perhaps,
> That love like youth is wasted on the young.

I must credit the great mind of George Bernard Shaw for the *last* line. He originally said, "Youth is so wonderful. It is a pity to waste it on children." Shaw was a rare and ingenious man and I would advise any lyrist to seek a librettist or playwright who stands as tall as Mr. Shaw. The playwright does make a difference for the lyrist. He sets the tone and the level for the lyrics. Of all the songs I have written, I am probably proudest of the lyrics for *Our Town*, thanks to the original genius of Thornton Wilder.

Now, the give-and-take of collaboration is pure joy for me, and I have never worked on a song that I didn't enjoy writing. But now and again there are intense discussions about certain rhyming patterns, and Jimmy Van Heusen and I had one of our best over writing the second half-chorus for "The Second Time Around"

> Love's more comft'able
> The second time you fall,
> Like a friendly home
> The second time you call.
>
> Who can say, what led us to this miracle we found?
>
> There are those who'll bet
> Love comes but once, and yet,
> I'm, oh, so glad we met
> THE SECOND TIME AROUND!

Van Heusen, who is a purist (his years with Johnny Burke did that), didn't like the sound of *t* at the end of the word. He would not have argued against the softness of a rhyme like *when, then, again,* but the *t* bothered him in *yet.* I sang the last eight bars of the song over and over to prove to him that it didn't grate on the ear and that it was *singable.* I finally won my point by quoting (I should say *singing*) from "Accustomed to Her Face":

> I was serenely independent and content
> Before we met.
> Surely I could always be that way again, and yet. . . .

Van Heusen agreed. The lyrics did sing.

This same singability was found in, "The Tender Trap."

We had the title from the MGM film, and we were writing at the behest of Frank Sinatra. I went to the typewriter.

At the instant I heard the word *trap* I heard the word *snap*, and the song was practically written. I typed:

> You see a pair of laughing eyes
> And suddenly you're sighing sighs,
> You're thinking nothing's wrong,
> You string along, boy, then snap!

I was about to add the title with the line

> You're in the tender trap!

But the rhythm of the words led me to add:

Those eyes, those sighs, they're part of THE TENDER TRAP!

It also added four extra bars to what is ordinarily an eight-bar section of a thirty-two bar song. So in twelve bars we have *eyes/sighs*, *wrong/along*, and *snap/trap*.

You're hand in hand beneath the trees
And soon there's music in the breeze,
You're acting kind of smart,
Until your heart just goes whap!
Those trees, that breeze, they're part of THE TENDER TRAP!

In the second twelve bars we have the sounds of *trees/breeze*, *smart/heart*, and *whap/trap*.

Since the twenty-four bars have a schottische feel, the professional lyrist will almost intuitively go to a legato or broader singing line. And so:

> Some starry night,
> When her kisses make you tingle,
> She'll hold you tight
> And you'll hate yourself for be-ing sing-le.

In these four lines I rhymed *night/tight,* single-syllable words, and *tingle/single,* double-syllable words, all adding interest for the listener.

> Then all at once it seems so nice,
> The folks are throwing shoes and rice,
> You hurry to a spot,
> That's just a dot on the map!
> You wonder how it all came about,
> It's too late now, there's no getting out,
> You fell in love, and love—is THE TENDER TRAP!

In the last sixteen bars (we added a four-bar tag for the ending) we have the sounds of *nice/rice, spot/dot,* and *map/trap.* I must also tell you that Van Heusen and I wrote this song at about one a.m. in the Hollywood Hills above the Hollywood Freeway. And since there are not too many practical rhymes for *trap,* we were so pleased to come up with "You hurry to a spot/That's just a dot, on the map" with the familiar bass notes in the left hand from Van Heusen. I also call your attention to the architecture of the music, which makes the lyrics conform. It is pure and exact. (To illustrate this point, I once asked Van Heusen to give me a grace note to add a little *But if* to a line. He stared at me and said, "I will write another melody for you.")

Jimmy Van Heusen is one of those rare composers. He knows how to bend his music to work with the lyrics. But he also knows *when* to do it.

I cannot emphasize the importance of singability above all other considerations, even when incorrect phrases are used:

> I have spurs that jingle jangle jingle
> As I go riding merrily along,
> And they say, Oh, ain't you glad you're single
> And that song Oh ain't so very far from wrong?

The incomparable Frank Loesser knew "ain't so very far from right" was correct, but "ain't so very far from wrong" sounded better. More important, it *sang* better.

One of my favorite examples of choosing sound over sense is in the lyrics of the great standard *Dark-town Strutters Ball.* There is an urgency in almost every line:

I'll be down to get you in a taxi, honey.
You better be ready by half past eight.
Now, honey, don't be late.
I wanna be there when the band starts playing.

And remember when we get there, honey,
Two steps we're gonna have them all.
We're gonna dance off both our shoes,
When they play "The Jelly-Roll Blues"
Tomorrow night, at the Dark-town Strutters Ball!

Now think about coming to the phrase "Tomorrow night" after all that urgency. Yet it displays a magic in matching words and music that is beyond sense, beyond intellectualizing, beyond anything.

Irving Berlin created perfect singability when he wrote:

And if I ever lost you, how much would I cry?
How deep is the ocean, how high is the sky?

Given his need to rhyme *sky* and that the number of possible rhymes is quite large, the magic is matching it with the word *cry*. It almost forces you to cry.

Oscar Hammerstein knew what he was doing when he wrote:

The corn is as high
As an elephant's eye

Obviously, a giraffe's eye would have been even higher, but don't try to sing:

The corn is as high
As a giraffe's eye

It doesn't quite sing the notes.

Gus Kahn, one of the great lyrists and a personal idol of mine, once sang "Carolina in the Morning" to a music publisher:

Nothing could be finer
Than to be in Carolina
in the mo-o-or-ning!

The publisher stopped him with, "What kind of lyric is 'Mo-o-or-ning'?"

To which Gus Kahn sang, "It fits the no-o-o-otes!"

"Mommy, Where do songs come from?"

Another question most young songwriters ask is, How do you get ideas for your songs?

Explaining how a child is born would be easier because there at least nature has provided some rules. But when a song is being born, the songwriter has no rules to follow. Ideas can come from anywhere, at anytime. And the great songwriters are often just people who have seen something simple right in front of their noses. Let me illustrate with the story of another collaboration.

I recall how one of the great ambitions of my life was realized when Robert Emmet Dolan of Paramount Pictures called to say that Van Heusen and I were to write songs for a film to be called *Papa's Delicate Condition* (a polite way of saying papa was inebriated, or just plain drunk). It seems I had waited all of my life for that call.

I remember when all the other songwriters left the East to go west to write for films, I envied them only one thing—the chance they might write the score for a Fred Astaire film. And there I was, signed to do a score for Fred Astaire. You cannot imagine how exhalted I felt, how I smiled in the night, and how I all but danced on the furniture in anticipation. Van Heusen and I received the script, and we started to make a musical "breakdown" (i.e., find places for the musical numbers).

One evening after an ample dinner, Van Heusen stretched out on an ample couch (everything around him was ample), and I studied the script. After a while I asked, "Do you like the title 'Call Me Irresponsible'?"

Van Heusen as always said, "How do you mean, 'the title'?"

I replied, "Call me irresponsible, call me undependable, toss in unreliable, too. . . ."

Van Heusen stared at the ceiling for about five minutes, and then he displayed what I consider to be his awesome talent. With one finger, he picked out the notes for that famous melody (I hope) you already know.

Where did the title come from? It came directly from the script. The script was replete with the word *irresponsible*: "Isn't he irresponsible?" "My, what an irresponsible thing to do," etc. Hence the title. The word established the cadence for the lyrics, which in turn established the melodic structure. So we had:

> Call me irresponsible,
> Call me undependable,
> Throw in unreliable, too

Since the cadence of these three lines was a little stiff because we were using five-syllable words, we went to a broader lyric and melodic line:

> Do my foolish alibis bore you?
> Well, I'm not too clever. I just adore you.
>
> Call me unpredictable,
> Tell me I'm impractical,
> Rainbows I'm inclined to pursue.
>
> Call me irresponsible,
> Yes, I'm undependable,
> But it's undeniably true,
> I'm irresponsibly mad for you!

I turned to Van Heusen and said, "Let's switch *undependable* and *unreliable* at the top because *undependable* will never be heard again. We'll have *unreliable* to match with *undeniably true*, which is a more graceful sound to the ear." He understood, and the song was finished.

In 1952, Van Heusen and I were teamed again and assigned to do the score for Frank Sinatra's new film, *Hole in the Head*. One afternoon Van Heusen walked into our office looking like he needed a little intensive care—he had been out with Frank the night before. As softly as possible, he said, "Frank thinks we ought to try to come up with a song for him to sing to the little boy [young Eddie Hodges]." It must have been collaborative ESP because just the night before a bit of a rhyme had popped into my head:

> High hopes
> High apple-pie in the sky hopes

Just that. Nothing more.

Normally, Van Heusen and I would go right to work. But in his condition, he only managed to say, "I like that. Let me take it home and work on it."

He came back the next day, partially recovered (you don't recover from a Sinatra night-on-the-town in one day), and played a 2/4 "Great Day" kind of melody for me. It wasn't at all what I had in mind. "Forget it. Let me try again," he said, and came back the next day (almost recovered) and played a 2/4 "Hallelujah" melody. I said, "You know, Jimmy, maybe we shouldn't write this from the viewpoint of people, but rather, of animals." Having said "animals," I knew I had asked the writer of the single greatest animal song ever written to write an animal song.*

"I apologize," I said. "I don't mean animals (at which point I saw these ants marching single-file over the threshold of a bungalow at the studio), I mean insects."

"Insects?" he said incredulously.

I pointed to the ants. "Look at them! They must have a sense of fulfillment. Anyone watching those ants could learn something."

I did. And before long we had:

> Next time you're found
> With your chin on the ground,
> There's a lot to be learned,
> So just look around——(to vamp)

I'll pause between the verse and chorus for a moment to discuss the lyrist, his skills, and where they must lead. The professional lyrist can sit down to write a waltz, a march, a ballad, etc. The verse to "High Hopes" was written in stop time with the after-beat after each line. When it came to the line "Just look around"—the vamp which followed was a natural progression to the drama and the musical action leading to the first line of the chorus:

> Just what makes that little ol' ant
> Think he'll move that rubber tree plant?

I pause again to illustrate how lyrics and rhymes come to be. "Just what makes that little ol' ant" is the cadence, so the next line's cadence had to match the staccatolike cadence of "little ol'

---

* The Academy-Award-winning "Swingin' on a Star."

xxi

ant." I had never seen an ant near a rubber tree, let alone *move* a rubber tree. But it had to have the right singability (matching "rubber tree plant" with "little ol' ant").

So when someone asks "Where does a song come from?" just remember how a little collaborative ESP and open eyes can find the song:

> Just what makes that little ol' ant
> Think he'll move that rubber tree plant?
> Anyone knows an ant—can't—
> Move a rubber tree plant.
>
> But he's got HIGH HOPES
> He's got HIGH HOPES
> He's got high apple-pie in the sky hopes.
>
> So anytime you're gettin' low,
> 'Stead of lettin' go,
> Just remember that ant.
>
> Oops! There goes another rubber tree
> Oops! There goes another rubber tree
> Oops! There goes another rubber tree plant!

Another song idea came from the usual phone call saying "I need a song." It was Frank Sinatra again (thank goodness). He was about to do an album for Capitol Records, and he had the notion of doing a song about taking a flying trip.

Van Heusen and I just sat there for a while and kicked some titles around. Finally, we both agreed on "Come Fly with Me" as the most evocative, especially when sung by Frank Sinatra. Since in this case we had the title first, I went to the typewriter and started to type:

> COME FLY WITH ME!
> Let's fly! Let's fly away!
> If you can use some exotic views,
> There's a bar in far Bombay,
> COME FLY WITH ME!
> Let's fly! let's fly away!

I often tell people that I don't write a song, so much as the song writes me. The above lyrics, in the time of the normal eight, eight,

eight, and eight, is a twelve-bar phrase. But Van Heusen and I never counted bars unless there was an uneven number to give us pause. I believe these lyrics brought forth from Van Heusen one of his most provocative, most original, and most unique compositions. (To give you some notion of how far we had come in the area of censorship, we were worried about using the line, or rather the rhyme, "If you can use some exotic booze," which is a far superior line for Frank Sinatra. We were afraid that the record would be barred from some stations, so we asked Frank to sing "views" on the recording and use "booze" in his act. Sinatra being Sinatra, he sang "booze.")

Let me also point out the line "There's a bar, in far Bombay." In the writing of any lyric, the occasional inner rhyme always makes for a more graceful sound. Hence, wherever you can have an inner rhyme, go for it!

> Come fly with me
> We'll float down to Peru
> In llama land, there's a one-man band
> And he'll toot, his flute, for you
> Come fly with me
> Let's take off in the blue!

Again, because we had the "notey" melody, we came back to the bridge and went for the broad legato line:

> Once I get you up there!
> Where the air is rare-ified
> We'll just glide, starry-eyed.
>
> Once I get you up there!
> I'll be holding you so near,
> You may hear angels cheer,
> 'Cause we're together.
>
> Weather-wise, it's such a lovely day!
> Just say the words and we'll beat the birds
> Down to Acapulco Bay.
>
> It's perfect for a flying honey-moon, they say,
> COME FLY WITH ME!
> Let's fly! Let's fly away!

Coming out of the bridge:

> Angels cheer 'cause we're together

Matching the closing word with the opening word of the next section always produces a graceful sound. My favorite example of this sound is in the lyric to "I Only Have Eyes for You," when the immortal Al Dubin wrote:

> I don't know if we're in a garden
> Or on a crowded avenue. You
>
> Are here, so am I,
> Maybe millions of people go by,
> But they all disappear from view,
> And I only have eyes for you!

Absolutely impeccable matching of words and music.

The words must marry the music

I cannot stress the vital importance of the music matching the words. And while it is achieved through collaboration between the composer and lyrist, often they are not the only people invovled in the writing of a song.

For example, Jimmy Van Heusen and I were once called to the Universal Studios to meet with Ross Hunter in order to discuss a film to be called *Thoroughly Modern Millie.* All the way out to the studio Van Heusen and I tried to think of a substitute title for this film, which was going to star the wonderful Julie Andrews. We felt they certainly couldn't call it *Thoroughly Modern Millie.* Sing it? You could hardly speak it! But we knew we were doomed when we got to Ross Hunter's office and he leaped to his feet with joy and shouted, "Isn't that the catchiest title?"

We went home depressed. Just as Alan Jay Lerner knew he would not rhyme Camelot (swam a lot? ate ham a lot? etc.), I knew that I wouldn't rhyme Millie, no matter what. Think of my options: silly, Willy, Piccadilly, etc. So we wrote a song and used the actual title just once, at the very end:

> So beat the drums, 'cause here comes
> Thoroughly modern Millie, now!

Came the fateful day. We went back to Universal and demonstrated the song for Ross Hunter and the famed Broadway director and choreographer, Joe Layton. They were both delighted. Ross Hunter leaped to his feet to shout his approval (I loved Ross Hunter, leaps and all). Joe Layton was also quite happy. Jimmy and I felt we had completed a very difficult assignment, the title song for a film called *Thoroughly Modern Millie*.

A few weeks later we were called back to Universal Studios to play the song for the director of the film, George Roy Hill. This time I really "leaned in" when I sang the song. When I finished, George Roy said, "Very, very good."

I said, "You don't like this song, Mr. Hill."

To which he said, "How could I not like a song by Sammy Cahn and James Van Heusen?"

I pause here with some most important advice to the future lyrist and/or composer. You must learn how to handle an honest rejection. A man has a right not to like everything you write. At one time when someone used to turn down a song of mine, I felt as though I was literally being kicked in the stomach. It hurt so much. Now, when someone isn't quite happy, I start to leave. I don't even want to discuss the why of it. I'm off to try to bring back something that will please the buyer.

Van Heusen and I went back to the drawing board. Funny enough, during the writing I felt that Van Heusen, who is the most relentless striver for originality in his composition, was fighting the natural, old-fashioned sound the song and the film required and the very sound that George Roy Hill was probably expecting. So I said, "Jimmy, let's try to write the kind of a song that sounds like it has already been written."

Before long we had:

> Everything today is thoroughly modern
> (*Old-fashioned musical sound*)
> Everything today makes yesterday slow
> (*Old-fashioned musical sound*)
>
> It's not insanity, says *Vanity Fair*
> In fact it's stylish to raise your skirts
>   and bob your hair (*music echoes*)
>
> In a rumble seat the world is so cozy
> (*Old-fashioned musical sound*)

And that tango dance they wouldn't allow
(*Old-fashioned musical sound*)

Good-bye good goody girl, I'm changing and how
So beat the drums, 'cause here comes
Thoroughly modern Millie, now!

Having finished the song, we now set about listening to it—even more carefully than the people we were going to play it for would listen to it. I said, "Jimmy, that dah-dle-dah-dle-dah-dle-ah sound is so infectious. Why don't I add a lyric for it?"

Typically, Van Heusen replied, "Be my guest."

Everything today is thoroughly modern
(Check your personality)
Everything today makes yesterday slow
(Better face reality)

In a rumble seat the world is so cozy
(If the boy is kissable)
And that tango dance they wouldn't allow
(Now is quite permissible)

I'm so pleased to say that the words in parentheses now became as important as the lyric itself.

Having finished two choruses, we needed a verse. Now, all verses, to quote an old music man, are simply, "And that's why I say. . . ." But verses are enormous fun, and many of them are as famous as their choruses. And because of a rhyme I'll come to shortly, this verse became quite important:

There are those, I suppose,
Think we're mad, heaven knows
The world has gone to rack and ruin.

What we think is chic, unique,
And quite adorable.

We first tried:

They like to yell is hell
And most deplorable.

Van Heusen, ever the moralist, said we'd never get away with *hell* from Julie Andrews, so we tried one or two more ideas. Happily, we soon hit upon:

> They think is odd, and Sod-
> om and Gomorrah-able—but the fact is—

Needless to say, George Roy Hill loved the new version, and Ross Hunter leaped to his feet to shout his approval. Now, not only was the impossible song written with singability, and not only did the words and music match, but they all matched the film.

I learned two valuable lessons from this experience: (1) The importance of honest rejection. (2) I could make an unsingable song into one that is *highly* singable.*

Another title song, "Pocketful of Miracles," had problems of a different nature. It was rhymable and singable, but it was also too close to a song that Jimmy Monaco had written with Johnny Burke called "Pocketful of Dreams":

> I'm no millionaire,
> But I'm not the type to care,
> 'Cause I've got a pocketful of dreams.

Van Heusen and I were in New York working on a musical when the phone rang. It was Frank Capra, the director I had worked with for the song "High Hopes" and the man who had won every award they give for film directing. He was calling to say he had completed a film called *Pocketful of Miracles*, and he needed a title song. My mental card index of song titles immediately flashed to "Pocketful of Dreams." Regretfully, I knew I'd have to say no to my close friend, but I didn't turn down the idea right away. I suggested that since the film was finished, he didn't need a title song. How would he get it into the film anyway? But Capra pleaded with me to see the film that night at the Loew's Sheridan in the Village.

That night Van Heusen, who was enthusiastic about the assignment, and I went to see the film, which starred Glenn Ford, Bette Davis, and Hope Lange and was based on Damon Runyon's story "Apple Annie." It was a charming film, but I was still troubled by

---

* ASCAP (The American Society of Composers, Authors and Publishers) cited it for being one of *the* most performed songs in one quarter!

the title being so similar to another song. (This is the sort of problem I've had to live with on other occasions, too. For instance, when I had to write a song about Chicago, I knew there was a song called "Chicago," a standard, so I wrote "My Kind of Town [Chicago Is]." While I know you cannot copyright a title, I wouldn't have written "Day by Day" knowing there was another "Day by Day." I wouldn't have written "New York, New York" knowing there was another "New York, New York," because both titles would be vitiated. When the monitor at ASCAP hears one of those titles, which song title would be credited?) But finally Van Heusen and Capra appealed to our friendship, and I agreed to give the song a try.

I began by asking myself, what is the opposite of dreams? Practicality! And so:

> Practicality
> Doesn't int'rest me,
> Love the life that I lead.
> I've got a pocketful of miracles
> And with a pocketful of miracles
> One tiny miracle a day is all I need!
>
> Troubles more or less
> Bother me, I guess,
> When the sun doesn't shine,
> But there's that pocketful of miracles
> And with a pocketful of miracles
> The world's a bright and shiny apple that's mine all mine!

A couple of quick comments on the above. In writing a title song I always try to use the title as often as possible, almost to the point of redundancy ("Thoroughly Modern Millie" being the exception to the rule). Also, in this lyric, it was a good idea to introduce *apple*, which plays such an important part in the film.

Then, because of the Christmas atmosphere that pervades the end of the film, we wrote:

> I hear sleigh bells ringing,
> Smack! In the middle of May
> I go around, like there's snow around.
> I feel so good it's Christmas every day.

Life's a carousel,
Far as I can tell,
And I'm riding for free,
So if you're down and out of miracles,
I've got a pocketful of miracles,
And there'll be miracles enough for you and me!

We listened to the song when it was finished, and I said to Van Heusen, "I don't like it very much."

Quick to take offense, he asked, "Well, what's wrong?"

It was the melody. It started with a downbeat before the first note:

(Boom) Practicality
(Boom) Doesn't int'rest me

I said, "You need a choreographer for this song," and I dropped my shoulder before *practicality* and before *doesn't int'rest me*. So we examined the problem. Then Van Heusen said, "Suppose we put a word in to replace the downbeat."

Real practicality
Sure doesn't int'rest me

I listened and said, "Now I like it even less." So we sat and we sat. Then I said, "Suppose we say,"

Pee-rac-ti-cal-ity
Dee-uz-n't int'rest me

Van Heusen said, "What the hell does that mean?"

I said, "I don't know what it means, but if everyone wonders, at least we'll have their attention. And if two people question it [a constant rule of mine], I'll change it."

Well, the song went in, and from that day to this, no one has asked what it means. The song was placed in the film under the main title and in different places in the film. It went on to be nominated for an Academy Award and was recorded by Frank Sinatra. I never hear it without thinking how glad I am that I "neatened it up" because the song is one of my happiest copyrights.

A Styne is more than a beer mug

Before I go any further in singing the praises of my relationship with Jimmy Van Heusen, I must tell you about another, equally talented composer I have had the good fortune to work with on many occasions.

Jule Styne can match music to words as well as any composer I know. And over the many years we wrote songs together, Jule never ceased to surprise me in the way he would come up with an idea for a song. For example, Jule and I were once in the offices of the Edwin H. Music Company. It was one of the hottest days in the history of Los Angeles. After the meeting, I asked Jule, "Why don't we drive to the beach to cool off?"

He said, typically, "Why don't we stay here and write a winter song?"

I went to the typewriter, reflected for an instant or two on the weather, and typed:

Oh! The weather outside is frightful

Notice how I set the cadence with the first line, a key to successful rhyming.

Oh! The weather outside is frightful
But the fire is so delightful
And since we've no place to go,
LET IT SNOW! LET IT SNOW! LET IT SNOW!

I gave these four lines (a form I later came to know as a quatrain) to Jule Styne. He went to the piano and started to noodle some different melodic lines to accommodate the cadence. This was the moment when collaboration became vital. If Styne needed to add a word to bring about a rhythmic pattern he liked or needed to drop a word for the same reason, I would make the changes to suit whatever melodic line we both agreed upon. Once we had agreed on the melody, I think you may know how I continued:

It doesn't show signs of stopping
And I brought some corn for popping,
The lights are turned 'way down low.
LET IT SNOW! LET IT SNOW! LET IT SNOW!

When we finally kiss good-night,
How I'll hate going out in the storm!
But if you'll really hold me tight
All the way home I'll be warm.

The fire is slowly dying
And, my dear, we're still good-bye-ing,
But as long as you love me so,
LET IT SNOW! LET IT SNOW! LET IT SNOW!

In this instance the lyric triggered the subsequent melody. When I began my lyric-writing career with Saul Chaplin, the words and music came almost simultaneously, with the lyrics a few lines ahead of the melody. And again with James Van Heusen, the lyrics came a few lines ahead of the melody. Collaborations, like collaborators, differ. And the method by which you get to the final song is not as important as the song itself.

Another fascinating case in point was my collaboration with Jule Styne on the score for *High Button Shoes*. We needed a song for the young girl who had to make a decision between two suitors. I came to Jule with the following lines:

I'm betwixt and between
Have to make my mind up which way to lean
Shall I stop? shall I go?
I simply must make my mind up!

I'm between and betwixt
Running in a race that someone has fixed
Is it to? Is it fro?
I wish I knew how I'll wind up!

Jule Styne came up with a really stirring 2/4 show tune, the kind Cole Porter has in every score (e.g., "Just One of Those Things," "From This Moment On," etc.) We rushed to the choreographer, Jerome Robbins, with the song. He listened and said, "You can't have this kind of a 2/4 show tune in an old-fashioned show like *High Button Shoes*! Are you both crazy?"
We knew he was right and sadly discarded the notion. Later however, Robbins remembered the tune when he was directing

Gypsy and suggested to Stephen Sondheim that he have Jule Styne play him the 2/4 song that never got into *High Button Shoes*. Jule did. Now, go back to the lyrics of "Betwixt and Between" and sing the melody of "Everything's Coming Up Roses." I'll always feel I had a part in the writing of that song.

Earlier I discussed the importance of singability in regard to incorrect phrases. In another song written for *High Button Shoes*, "You're My Girl," I had to contend with singability by working with an *impure* rhyme. Suffice it to say, if I could undo any impure rhyme, I would do it in an instant, or at least I would try.

In the case of "You're My Girl," there is a hidden impure rhyme so imperceptible that I am not sure that anyone has ever caught it, or will catch it:

> YOU'RE MY GIRL,
> The boys all know,
> YOU'RE MY GIRL,
> I've told them so.
>
> You should have seen how their faces fell,
> When they were wishing me well.
> They called me a lucky guy
> And I couldn't hide a feeling of pride.
>
> YOU'RE MY GIRL,
> I've chosen you,
> To be mine
> My whole life through.
>
> And if this heart of mine had a voice,
> You'd hear it second my choice.
>
> You're what I've waited for
> And YOU'RE MY GIRL!

I often use impure rhymes for comedic purposes. In that situation the impure rhyme is working for you. For instance, there really isn't any pure rhyme for *pregnant*, so in writing special lyrics about a man and his wife (she had eight children by him) I used (sung to the bridge of "It's Been a Long, Long Time"):

> It seems the only times she ever got indignant
> Were the times her husband made her—prig-nant!

Special lyrics can be fun because they almost create their own language. You find yourself using words in a way that would normally be overlooked, or in a way they would never be used at all. A few years back when I was asked to write some special lyrics for Jule Styne to the tune of "I Can't Get Started with You," I had to find a rhyme for the word *music*. After trying and trying, I couldn't find a pure rhyme, so I used (sung to the bridge):

> You've welcomed me, me most enthusic'ly
> Me, me most effusic'ly
> Me, loved me most music'ly
> I'm so pleased I could die.

(E. Y. Harburg was a master of this sort of impeccably literate wit, and a study of his lyrics and poems is an education in rhyming.)

When I write an actual song, not special lyrics, I agonize over the thought of using an impure rhyme. Often the process of "neatening up" that one troublesome rhyme can be more time-consuming than writing the entire piece.

I am always amazed when I am confronted with song lyrics that try to rhyme *door* and *go.* Recently a song I heard rhymed *frantic* and *panic*! Obviously in the first instance the writer heard *go* and *do'*. But what the writer heard in the rhyme *frantic* and *panic*, I'm not sure.

There are endless impure rhymes like *forever* and *together*, but it's not enough for such words to sound *like* a rhyme, they must *be* a rhyme. *Whither flows the river* sounds like a rhyme, but it isn't.

I have used the expression "neaten up" and have elaborated at length on how important it is to really go over and over the lyric. Sing it until no word sticks in the mouth. Be sure that every word, every phrase, every syllable sings effortlessly. And when you have the "hook," the section you want them to remember most—make sure it stands out.

In my song "It's Magic" I "neatened up" the song by inserting a rhyme that vastly improved the lyric:

> You sigh, the song begins,
> You speak and I hear violins,
> IT'S MAGIC.

> The stars desert the skies
> And rush to nestle in your eyes,
> IT'S MAGIC.

I first had:

> I need no magic wand,
> No mystic charm,
> I'm in a world beyond
> When we are arm in arm.

It became:

> Without a golden wand
> Or mystic charms
> Fantastic things be*gin*
> When I am *in* your arms.

It is almost what it was, but it is so much neater. And above all, it sings so much better. When you have finished a lyric you are pleased with, just put it aside. It will not self-destruct. Then try to redo it. Rewrite it completely. You can always go back to the original, but at least you will have repeated the great pleasure and adventure of creativity.

Good professional writers are rarely satisfied. The stereotyped image of the composer and lyrist arguing probably began with an effort by the two to "neaten up" a melody or lyric.

Before Jule Styne and I wrote a new song, he would warm up with a song we wrote together, "The Christmas Waltz":

> Frosted window panes,
> Candles gleaming inside,
> Painted candy canes on the tree;

> Santa's on his way,
> He's filled his sleigh with things,
> Things for you and me.

Styne and I debated the use of the word *toys* instead of *things* but felt *toys* would make it more a children's song, while *things* might make it a bit more adult.

It's that time of year,
When the world falls in love,
Ev'ry song you hear seems to say:

"Merry Christmas,
May your New Year dreams come true."

Then we picked up the feel of a real Viennese waltz at the end:

And this song of mine,
In three-quarter time,
Wishes you and yours
The same thing too.

Styne and I were delighted because the song seemed to write itself and we smiled at each other over the happy outcome. Then suddenly I said, "I'll have to 'neaten it up.' There's an impure rhyme—*mine* and *time*." Styne insisted it sounded right, but I convinced him to try again. We got:

And this song sublime,
In three-quarter time,

Let the church bells chime
In three-quarter time,

And this merry rhyme
In three-quarter time

After a number of grimaces, we both felt the best choice was to go with the lyric that was most singable:

And this song of mine,
In three-quarter time,
Wishes you and yours
The same thing too.

Frank Sinatra went on to record that song three different times, and many other artists since have also recorded it.

Sometimes out of necessity you have to stretch for the impure rhyme, but sometimes depending on what singability or context dictate, you may choose not to rhyme at all!

During World War II Jule Styne and I wrote a song that many people say stirred simultaneous emotions of romanticism and patriotism. Many of the fan letters I received from men and women about this song said it helped them convey what they were trying to express in their letters to their boyfriends or girlfriends. The song was called "I'll Walk Alone," and it was written for a film produced by Charles K. Feldman called *Follow the Boys*, which starred Dinah Shore and George Raft. It fulfilled one great goal for me. I always envied Jule Styne his great copyright "I Don't Want to Walk Without You, Baby," with lyrics by the legendary Frank Loesser. Now, if you think about it, these two songs are saying the same thing. I gave Jule the first lines:

> I'LL WALK ALONE
> Because, to tell you the truth, I'll be lonely.

Instead of rhyming the word *lonely*, which has very few really rhymable words (e.g., *only*), we thought it would be more meaningful to repeat the word *lonely* and left it unrhymed:

> I don't mind being lonely
> When my heart tells me you
> Are lonely too.

> I'LL WALK ALONE,
> They'll ask me why and I'll tell them I'd rather;
> There are dreams I must gather,
> Dreams we fashioned the night
> You held me tight.

In the second eight I had rhymed *rather* and *gather* because it was fresh-sounding and because the thought of gathering dreams led to "fashioned the night you held me tight." In a reversal of the long notes following the eighth notes, we went into a bridge that was almost all eighth notes and is very neatly rhymed throughout:

> I'll always be near you,
> Wherever you are,
> Each night in ev'ry prayer.

> If you call I'll hear you,
> No matter how far;
> Just close your eyes and I'll be there.

Please walk alone
And send your love and your kisses to guide me.
Till you're walking beside me,
I'LL WALK ALONE.

Of all the songs I have written, "I'll Walk Alone" is the only song that has sold over one million copies of sheet music. Not records. Sheet music. I consider it one of my proudest achievements. I remember a glow of pride watching a newsreel in a movie theater (this was before the days of television) that showed a foot-weary regiment that could have been sketched by Bill Mauldin marching into a French village. On a wall behind them someone had painted "I'll walk Cologne!"

"I'll Walk Alone" became popular in every English-speaking country, and, to repeat myself, I am very proud to have written it.

At one point when the war was winding down, I looked at Jule Styne and said, "We should have a song for when the boys come back."

That idea led us to a new song and brought up the question, What is a sixteen-bar song? The answer—half of a 32-bar song.

I looked at Jule and said, "How is this for an idea?"

Just kiss me once, then kiss me twice,
Then kiss me once again,
IT'S BEEN A LONG, LONG TIME.

I didn't realize that when I gave Jule the idea, I practically gave him the whole song. With true genius, he went to the piano and immediately picked out the melody.

Haven't felt like this, my dear,
Since can't remember when,
IT'S BEEN A LONG, LONG TIME.

You'll never know how many dreams
I dreamed about you
Or just how empty they all seemed
Without you

So kiss me once, then kiss me twice,
Then kiss me once again,
IT'S BEEN A LONG, LONG TIME.

When Jule Styne sat down to make his traditional three-line piano part, he said, "We've written a sixteen-bar song."

I said, "So?"

He said, "So let's write a verse so it will seem longer," and we did:

> Never thought that you would be
> Standing here so close to me.
> There's so much I feel that I should say,
> But words can wait until some other day, just . . .

And it was finished. We didn't sit down with the intention of writing a sixteen-bar song, but in this case it only took sixteen bars to say it all.

Another sixteen-bar song was from *Anchors Aweigh*, which has become a standard for jazz musicians. "I Fall in Love Too Easily," was introduced by the then idolized—and painfully thin—Frank Sinatra. The scene was the Hollywood Bowl. Looking every inch the handsome idol to every female present, he went to the piano and sang one chorus:

> I fall in love too easily,
> I fall in love too fast,
> I fall in love too terribly hard,
> For love to ever last.
>
> My heart should be well schooled
> 'Cause I've been fooled in the past,
>
> And still I fall in love too easily,
> I fall in love too fast.

This song was written one night in Palm Springs. When I sang the last line, Jule Styne looked over at me and said, "So. That's it." I know he felt we could have written on, but I felt I had said all there was to say, and if I had it to do over, I would stop right there again.

Over the many years of collaborating with Jule Styne and Jimmy Van Heusen, there was one distinction that set the two men apart. When I started this introduction, I asked the question, Which comes first—the words or the music? Well, there was one time when they came simultaneously.

Every lyric writer writes to a sort of dummy, or temporary, melody, one he uses until the composer takes over. But once the dummy melody became the final one. It was a Saturday night in New York City. Jule Styne and I each had suites in the Gotham Hotel on Fifth Avenue at 55th Street. It was sevenish when my sister Florence and her husand, Jules Goldberg, dropped by. Seeing me in my pajamas and robe, my sister asked, apprehensively, "Aren't you feeling well?"

"I'm feeling fine!"

"Then why aren't you dressed to go out? It's Saturday night!"

I replied, "Saturday night is for civilians. I can go out Sunday, Monday, Tuesday, Wednesday, Thursday, and Friday, but if you're in show business, Saturday night is the loneliest night in the week." They seemed to understand and left. I walked to the piano and in the key of F (I am always in the key of F), I picked out the dummy melody: *Da, da, da, da, da, da, da, da, da, da, da, da, da.* And a matching *da, da, da, da, da, da, da, da, da, da, da, da, da, da,* all the while singing to myself:

SATURDAY NIGHT IS THE LONELIEST NIGHT IN THE WEEK,
'Cause that's the night that my sweetie and I used to dance
    cheek to cheek.

Once more the title, which in this case is the entire opening line, was the cadence for the second line and for the entire song.

I waited patiently until ten-thirty for Jule Styne to return to the hotel. When he got in, I went to the piano and played the first two lines. He said, "It's marvelous. Let's finish it."

Van Heusen would have listened, looked at me with great contempt and suggested that he might write something vastly better— but which might not have sold. In any case, Styne went to the piano, and I went to my trusty portable typewriter.

Since we had the long eight-bar line of eighth notes, we went almost intuitively to the quarter notes and half notes for the next part:

> I don't mind Sunday night at all
> 'Cause that's the night friends come to call
> And Monday to Friday go fast
> And another week is past,

Then the welcome sound of returning to the first eight and eighth notes:

But SATURDAY NIGHT IS THE LONELIEST NIGHT
  IN THE WEEK,
I sing the song that I sang for the mem'ries I usually seek.

And picking up the sound of the second eight for the end of the song:

Until I hear you at the door,
Until you're in my arms once more,
SATURDAY NIGHT IS THE LONELIEST NIGHT IN THE WEEK.

A Special Word or Two

It seems that writing special lyrics for special occasions has been a preoccupation of mine for as long as I can remember. When I was unable to break down the barriers to the music publishers—and you must believe I tried—I turned to the next best thing: writing special material. I wrote for comics, jugglers, sword swallowers, belly dancers. . . . Put it this way. If it moved, I wrote for it. And I learned as I matched the skills of other great lyrists. To this day, I am still engaged in writing, and now also performing, special lyrics for special occasions. It is so rewarding to go over the lyrical trail of other lyric giants. It is rewarding to the ego as well as to the bank account. When I base special lyrics on my own songs, I am offering something unique: an author tailoring his own lyric to a very special occasion. For example, here is a song I wrote for the prestigious corporation, AT&T (sung to "Time After Time"):

TIME AFTER TIME
I take the normal dime
And try to make the normal call.
I hear the coin drop,
The tone begin and stop,
Then a lonely silence and that's all.
I only know what I know,
You guys owe me some dough,
And, chums, the sum's not very small
'Cause time after time
I've used more than one dime
And never made a call at all!

In writing that song, I displayed incredible control by not calling it "Dime After Dime," but it would have been too easy, and the joke would have been over before it started. Also, as a general rule, I try to use as much of the original lyric as possible. It makes the parody seem more special.

Once I was taken to South Africa to do an evening for the De Beers Diamond Company. I sang this special lyric to "Three Coins in the Fountain":

> Three rings on each finger,
> That would suit De Beers just fine.
> Three rings on each finger,
> Making every finger shine.
> Make them mine! Make them mine! Make them mine!

At an evening for the IBM Corporation (sung to the tune of "I Should Care"):

> IBM
> No initials are better.
> IBM
> Each a marvelous letter.

Recently Frank Sinatra called me and asked if I would think of an introduction for Cary Grant at the Friar's Man of the Year dinner held at the Waldorf in New York. I chose the incredibly beautiful "The Most Beautiful Girl in the World" by the legendary team of Richard Rodgers and Lorenz Hart.

At the long-awaited moment, Sinatra sang:

> The most beautiful man in the world
> Isn't me, No! Isn't Di-no, but as we know
> It's the man that we honor tonight.
>
> The most talented man in the world,
> Not John Gielgud, tho' he's real good, would he feel good
> With a Friar to his left and a Friar to his right?
> Cary is unique, handsome as a Greek.
> Ladies from his plots, they still have the lingering "hots."
>
> The most fabulous man in the world,
> Counting tall men, counting small men, counting all men,
> Who's the hero that all of us try to supplant?
> It's the one and only wonderful Cary Grant!

It was, I am pleased to say, a magic moment. Many were moved to tears, mainly Mr. Grant. It is also interesting to note that when Mr. Hart wrote the original lyrics to "The Most Beautiful Girl in the World," he didn't go for the rhyme three ways. He could have said:

> The most beautiful girl in the world
> Eats my candy, drinks my brandy, and she's handy.
> The most beautiful girl in the world!

Instead, he wrote:

> The most beautiful girl in the world
> Picks my ties out, eats my candy, drinks my brandy.
> The most beautiful girl in the world!

Happily, he didn't repeat the rhyme three times. There is a time when you can over-rhyme. What might work for parodies could hurt songs. For instance, I am told that Gershwin's original lyrics for "Someone to Watch over Me" were slightly different from those we've come to know:

> Altho' he may not be the man some
> Girls think of as hand-some,
> He's worth a king's ransom to me.

Gershwin changed it to:

> Altho' he may not be the man some
> Girls think of as hand-some,
> To my heart he carries the key.

This left the rhyme for *me* to use in the verse.

Writing lyrics, special or otherwise, is fun. In closing, I can only add that to understand how to rhyme, you must know the literature of songs and lyrics. You must try to know all of the lyrics by all of the lyrists. People often ask me if I know all of the lyrics I've ever written. Not only do I know all of my own lyrics, regular songs, and specials (which add up to the thousands), but I also know everyone else's songs. And I also know that people like Johnny Mercer, Mitchell Parish, and Hal David can quote verbatim first and second choruses and verses from almost as many songs as I can.

When I sat down to write this introduction I was tempted to begin with a lyric from a project I had worked on with Jimmy Van Heusen and a then-struggling Avery Corman. (Since writing *Kramer vs. Kramer*, Mr. Corman has stopped struggling.)

The project was called *Witch of the Rhymes*. It was a fable about a young girl who cannot do magic because she isn't really a witch. As in many a fable, her name is Serena. A young shepherd named Nicholas tells her that to do magic all she needs to know is the rhyme Abra-ca-dabra.

In closing, I'll leave you with that song, "It's Rhyme-able":

Verse: (As continued dialogue by Nicholas)
I'm sure that we all admire
That man who first discovered fire.
Indebted we ought to feel
To the man who invented the wheel.

Whatever their name, their fame will live thru time.

But a man that I would rate
As truly great,
Who wipes the others clearly off the slate

Is the man who helped to create—RHYME!

His face must have glowed
When he brought that happy sound out—and found out

Mat-cat, true-blue, sing-spring, love-dove

Chorus:

Any word at all is rhyme-able.
Rhyme-able! Rhyme-able!

Take a simple name like Nicholas.
You can rhyme it with ridich-olas
If you aren't too metich-olas

It will come out rhyme-able
If the rhythm's double-time-able *(double the rhythm)*

Happy words are always rhyme-able
And they're fun to do

Love-able, skies above-able,
Please-able, birds and bees-able,
Joy-fully, girl and boy-fully.

They're rhyme-able! Rhyme-able!
And when things aren't too sublime-able,
It's amazing what a rhyme or two can do for you!

Chorus: (2)

Any word at all is rhyme-able.
Rhyme-able! Rhyme-able!

When you're sad and near hys-tirical,
You will find by being lyrical,
You can bring about a miracle.

Think a thought that is rhyme-able
And a busted bell is chime-able *(sound of busted gong!)*

Try a word or two that's rhyme-able,
Change your point of view.

Tearfully, turns to cheer-fully,
Gloom-erous, turns to humor-ous,
Humor-ous, to resume-erous.

It's rhyme-able! Rhyme-able!
And the steepest hill is climb-able.
It's amazing what a rhyme or two can do for you!

So dear friends, I cannot think of a nicer closing line to introduce a dictionary of rhyme. I envy you the pleasure, the adventures, and the fun of discovery.

Beverly Hills
October 12, 1982

[NOTE: Be certain to read "How to Use This Book," which follows this Introduction.]

How to Use This Book

This dictionary has been organized to answer the obvious question, "What rhymes with _____?" The plan of organization requires you always to keep two facts in mind when you start looking for a rhyme: first, all the entries are based on an approximation of the *sound* rather than a literal dictionary spelling of the words included; second, it is a backwards, Alice-in-Wonderland dictionary because all the words are alphabetized by their *end sounds* rather than by their initial letters. If you read the detailed explanation of both these structural concepts and follow a few simple steps, you should have no trouble finding the list of rhyme words you seek.

For all these steps, begin with the word you need to rhyme and

1. Isolate its last *accented* vowel sound.

All rhymes are basically vowel sounds with consonants attached to them. The vowel sound is the dominant note, and any preceding or following consonant or syllable(s) is of secondary importance. Accordingly, this dictionary is divided into five primary sections: A E I O U.

Of course, no single sound exists for these vowel letters. In their pronunciation guides all standard dictionaries break each of the five vowels down into some pattern of specific variations, or what will be called subvowels. This dictionary has three subvowel sounds for *a*, two for *e*, two for *i*, five for *o*, and two for *u*—fourteen in all. So your next step is to turn to the table of contents and

2. Find the *subvowel* sound that matches the last accented vowel sound in your word.

The reason it is important to isolate the last *accented* subvowel sound in your word is because not all rhymes are of the simple *moon/June/spoon* variety. For example, when you have a word like *gratefully*, the *ful* and *ly* syllables really just form a secondary ending to the *grate* sound. It would be hopelessly confusing to list together in one subvowel section every word in the English language that ends with an *ly* sound. This dictionary is organized by primary, not secondary vowel sounds. To use it, you just lop off (for the time being) the secondary syllables and isolate the primary vowel sound (in this case the *ay* (or ā) sound of *grate*. If you have any difficulty placing the subvowel sound of your word, check it against the Pronunciation Key facing the Contents, on page v.

When you have found the right subvowel section for your rhyme word, the next step is to

3. Find the number of "sounds" in your rhyme word.

"Sound" in this dictionary refers to what we might call the business end of the rhyme word. For example, if you take the rhyme words *indicate/celebrate*, the rhyme sound is *ate*. It's a *single-sound* rhyme in a three-syllable word. Similarly, take the pair *stalking/talking*. The rhyme is *alking*, which is a *double-sound* rhyme in a two-syllable word. Finally, look at a pair like *peacable/greasable*. Here we have, once the initial consonant is discarded, a *triple-sound* rhyme, *easable*, in a three-syllable word.

To summarize this step, once you figure out how many rhyme sounds there are (1, 2, or 3) in the word you want to rhyme, you turn to the single-, double-, or triple-sound section of the subvowel group for that word. They are all to be found in the table of contents.

Now there are really only two steps left. Each of these single-, double-, and triple-sound subsections in the dictionary comprises a series of what will be called *rhyme endings* (in boldface type) followed by a list of words that share that rhyme ending. These rhyme endings are alphabetized, so the next step is to

4. Find the rhyme ending you need.

Now alphabetizing a "backwards" dictionary is a bit tricky. For example, the single-sound rhyme endings are alphabetized in this order: vowel sound + preceding consonant(s) (bō, dō, lō, etc.); vowel sound + following consonant(s) (ōd, ōf, ōl, etc.); then in the double- and triple-sound sections, primary vowel sound + secondary vowel sound(s) (ōs'ən, ōs'ĭs, ōsh'ən, etc.).

(NOTE: The preceding examples have been given in the phonetic transcription system used throughout this dictionary, which has been adapted from a standard dictionary pronunciation guide. All rhyme endings appear not only in this fashion but are also preceded by a familiar and easy-to-read, spelled-out approximation of the sound, e.g., oaf (ōf). But since the phonetic transcriptions are more consistently accurate, you are well advised to study the Pronunciation Key on p. v, facing the contents page, carefully before rhyme hunting.)

The final step after locating the subvowel sound and rhyme ending is to take the word you want to rhyme and

5. Look for the word list that has the same number of syllables.

All the word lists (with a handful of exceptions) are for one-, two-, or three-syllable words. Each list is indicated by a boldface **1**, **2**, or **3**. Some rhyming dictionaries go into long, polysyllabic word lists, but this book is aimed primarily at the amateur and professional lyric, jingle, or light-verse writer and not at the academic linguist or writer.

Each word list tries to include as many appropriate rhyme words as possible, but if any appear missing, it is inevitable rather than intentional. The notion of a complete and completely accurate rhyming dictionary is unlikely given the margin for doubt and difficulty involved. The whole question of regional or international variation in the pronunciation of words in English is a valid one, but probably has no place in a basic book like this. If you think a word is pronounced a certain way, you will surely find a word list in this book to go with it.

The best advice for using *The Songwriter's Rhyming Dictionary* is to take the time to read and perhaps reread this section, hunting down practice words until the organization becomes clear. If you are impatient, you can probably still do pretty well skimming the running heads in search of the rhyme ending you want.

Single ay (ā) sounds

As an old native-born Californian would say,
It's a most unusual day.

—"It's a Most Unusual Day," lyric by Harold
   Adamson, music by Jimmy McHugh

ay (ā)

1
a
bay
bray
clay
day
Fay
fray
gay
gray
(grey)
hay
(hey)
jay
Kay
lay
(lei)
may
nay
pay
play
pray
(prey)
ray
say
slay
(sleigh)
spay
spray
stay
stray

sway
they
tray
way
(weigh)
yea

2
abbé
André
archway
array
astray
away
beret
betray
birthday
bobsleigh
Bombay
bouquet
Broadway
byway
café
Cathay
chalet
chambray
chassé
cliché
convey
coupé
croquet
decay
delay

dismay
display
entrée
essay
fair play
fairway
Friday
gourmet
halfway
hallway
headway
heyday
highway
horseplay
hurray
inlay
lamé
Mayday
midday
Midway
mislay
Monday
nosegay
obey
okay
padre
parfait
parlay
passé
pathway
payday
portray
prepay

railway
relay
repay
risqué
roadway
runway
some way
stairway
stingray
subway
Sunday
survey
Thursday
today
touché
toupée
Tuesday
waylay
weekday

3
appliqué
attaché
breakaway
canapé
castaway
Chevrolet
Christmas
   Day
consommé
déclassé
disarray
disobey

3

divorcée
Easter Day
everyday
exposé
fiancé
getaway
holiday
Judgment
 Day
market day
matinee
Milky Way
Monterey
negligée
overlay
overplay
Photoplay
popinjay
protégé
resumé
rockaway
runaway
Santa Fe
Saturday
silver gray
stowaway
straightaway
underplay
waterway
wedding day
Wednesday
working day
yesterday

abe (āb)

1
Abe
Babe

3
astrolabe

ade (ād)

1
aid
(aide)

bade
blade
braid
(brayed)
fade
glade
grade
(grayed)
jade
laid
made
(maid)
neighed
paid
played
prayed
(preyed)
raid
shade
sleighed
spade
sprayed
stayed
(staid)
strayed
suede
trade
wade
(weighed)

2
afraid
arcade
blockade
bridesmaid
brigade
brocade
cascade
charade
conveyed
crocheted
crusade
decayed
degrade

delayed
dismayed
evade
forbade
handmade
homemade
housemaid
inlaid
invade
mermaid
milkmaid
nightshade
nursemaid
obeyed
old maid
parade
parleyed
(parlayed)
persuade
pervade
postpaid
prepaid
relayed
(relaid)
remade
repaid
sautéed
self-made
stockade
surveyed
unmade
unpaid

3
appliquéd
barricade
cavalcade
centigrade
dairymaid
disarrayed
escalade
escapade
everglade
lemonade
marinade

masquerade
orangeade
overpaid
overweighed
palisade
promenade
readymade
renegade
serenade
unafraid

afe (āf)

1
chafe
safe
strafe
waif

aig (āg)

1
Hague
plague
vague

age (āj)

1
age
cage
guage
page
rage
sage
stage
wage

2
assuage
backstage
engage
enrage
greengage
outrage
rampage
upstage

3

disengage
overage

aged (ājd)

1

aged
caged
gauged
paged
raged
staged
waged

2

assuaged
engaged
enraged
outraged
rampaged
upstaged

ake (āk)

1

ache
bake
brake
(break)
cake
drake
fake
flake
lake
make
quake
rake
sake
snake
stake
(steak)
take
wake

2

awake
backache

beefsteak
clambake
daybreak
earache
earthquake
forsake
fruitcake
grubstake
headache
heartache
heartbreak
intake
keepsake
mandrake
mistake
muckrake
namesake
nutcake
opaque
outbreak
partake
remake
shortcake
sweepstake
toothache

3

overtake
rattlesnake
undertake

aked (ākt)

1

ached
baked
braked
faked
flaked
quaked
raked
snaked
staked

ale (āl)

1

ale
(ail)
bale
(bail)
dale
fail
flail
frail
gale
hale
(hail)
jail
male
(mail)
nail
pale
(pail)
quail
rail
sale
(sail)
scale
shale
snail
stale
tale
(tail)
trail
vale
(vail)
(veil)
wale
(whale)
(wail)
Yale

2

avail
bobtail
blackmail
Clydesdale
cocktail
curtail

detail
dovetail
exhale
fantail
guardrail
handrail
hangnail
impale
inhale
pigtail
prevail
regale
resale
telltale
thumbnail
toenail
wholesale

3

Abigail
fairy tale
fingernail
monorail
nightingale
tattletale

aled (āld)

1

ailed
baled
(bailed)
failed
flailed
hailed
jailed
mailed
nailed
paled
quailed
railed
sailed
scaled
tailed
trailed
veiled

wailed
(whaled)

2 ───────
availed
bobtailed
blackmailed
cocktailed
curtailed
derailed
detailed
exhaled
impaled
inhaled
pigtailed
prevailed
regaled
retailed
unveiled

ame (ām)

1 ───────
aim
blame
came
claim
dame
fame
flame
frame
game
lame
maim
name
same
shame
tame

2 ───────
acclaim
aflame
became
defame
disclaim
doorframe

exclaim
inflame
nickname
proclaim
reclaim
rename
selfsame
surname

3 ───────
counterclaim
overcame

amed (āmd)

1 ───────
aimed
blamed
claimed
famed
framed
maimed
named
shamed
tamed

2 ───────
acclaimed
ashamed
defamed
disclaimed
exclaimed
inflamed
nicknamed
proclaimed
reclaimed
renamed

ane (ān)

1 ───────
bane
brain
cane
(Cain)
chain

crane
Dane
drain
feign
gain
grain
Jane
lane
(lain)
Maine
(main)
(mane)
pain
(pane)
plane
(plain)
rein
(reign)
(rain)
sane
slain
Spain
sprain
stain
strain
swain
train
twain
vane
(vain)
(vein)
wane

2 ───────
abstain
again
airplane
arraign
attain
campaign
champagne
Champlain
chow mein
cocaine
contain

detain
disdain
domain
explain
humane
insane
migraine
mundane
obtain
ordain
pertain
profane
propane
refrain
regain
remain
retain
restrain
seaplane
tearstain
terrain
unchain

3 ───────
aeroplane
ascertain
Charlemagne
entertain
featherbrain
hurricane
hydroplane
inhumane
preordain
reordain
scatterbrain
sugar cane
windowpane

aned (ānd)

1 ───────
brained
caned
chained
drained
feigned

gained
grained
pained
planed
rained
(reigned)
sprained
stained
strained
trained
waned

2

abstained
arraigned
attained
campaigned
contained
detained
disdained
explained
maintained
ordained
pertained
profaned
regained
remained
restrained
retained
unchained

3

ascertained
entertained
featherbrained
preordained
scatterbrained

ange (ānj)

1

change
grange
mange
range
strange

2

arrange
derange
estrange
exchange
shortchange

3

interchange
prearrange
rearrange

aint (ānt)

1

ain't
faint
paint
quaint
saint
taint

2

acquaint
complaint
constraint
repaint
restraint

ape (āp)

1

ape
cape
crepe
drape
gape
grape
nape
rape
scape
scrape
shape
tape

2

escape
landscape

red tape
reshape
shipshape

aped (āpt)

1

aped
draped
gaped
raped
scraped
shaped
taped

2

escaped
red-taped
reshaped

air (ār)

1

air
bear
(bare)
blare
care
chair
Clare
dare
fare
(fair)
flare
(flair)
glare
hair
(hare)
heir
lair
mare
pair
(pear)
(pare)
prayer
rare
scare
share

snare
spare
square
stair
(stare)
swear
tear
there
(their)
where
(ware)
(wear)

2

affair
armchair
aware
beware
compare
declare
despair
éclair
elsewhere
footwear
forbear
(forebear)
glassware
hardware
horsehair
impair
Mayfair
mohair
nightmare
nowhere
Pierre
prepare
repair
somewhere
Voltaire
warfare
welfare

3

anywhere
billionaire
debonair

Delaware
everywhere
millionaire
overbear
questionnaire
rocking chair
savoir faire
solitaire
thoroughfare
unaware
underwear

aired (ārd)

1

aired
bared
cared
dared
flared
glared
scared
shared
snared
spared
squared
stared

2

compared
declared
ensnared
fair-haired
gray-haired
impaired
prepared
repaired

ace (ās)

1

ace
base
(bass)
brace
case
chase

face
grace
lace
mace
pace
place
race
space
trace
vase

2

birthplace
bookcase
cardcase
debase
deface
disgrace
displace
efface
embrace
erase
grimace
misplace
paleface
replace
shoelace
showcase
staircase
suitcase

3

angel face
baby face
Boniface
commonplace
hiding place
interlace
interspace
resting place
steeplechase

aced (āst)

1

baste
(based)

braced
cased
chaste
(chased)
faced
graced
haste
laced
paste
(paced)
placed
raced
spaced
taste
traced
waste
(waist)

2

debased
encased
lambaste
posthaste
toothpaste
two-faced

3

aftertaste
angel-faced
baby-faced
dirty-faced
freckle-faced
interlaced

ate (āt)

1

ate
bate
(bait)
crate
date
eight
fate
freight
gate
(gait)

great
(grate)
hate
Kate
late
mate
pate
plate
rate
sate
skate
slate
state
strait
(straight)
trait
weight
(wait)

2

abate
await
belate
berate
checkmate
classmate
collate
create
debate
deflate
elate
estate
helpmate
inflate
innate
instate
lightweight
negate
ornate
outdate
placate
playmate
postdate
predate
prorate

8

rebate
relate
sedate
stalemate
testate
translate

3

abdicate
adulate
advocate
aggravate
aggregate
agitate
alienate
allocate
animate
bantamweight
calculate
candidate
captivate
celebrate
celibate
circulate
complicate
concentrate
confiscate
congregate
consummate
contemplate
correlate
cultivate
decorate
dedicate
delegate
demonstrate
depredate
designate
desolate
devastate
deviate
dislocate
dominate
duplicate
educate

elevate
emigrate
emulate
estimate
fabricate
fascinate
featherweight
federate
formulate
generate
graduate
granulate
heavyweight
hesitate
hyphenate
illustrate
imitate
immigrate
implicate
incubate
indicate
infiltrate
innovate
instigate
insulate
interstate
intimate
intricate
inundate
irrigate
irritate
isolate
legislate
liberate
liquidate
litigate
lubricate
mediate
meditate
moderate
motivate
navigate
obligate
operate
opiate

orchestrate
ordinate
overrate
overstate
overweight
paperweight
penetrate
permeate
populate
procreate
propagate
punctuate
radiate
recreate
(re-create)
regulate
reinstate
relegate
relocate
segregate
separate
simulate
situate
speculate
stimulate
stipulate
syncopate
tolerate
triplicate
understate
underweight
validate
ventilate
welterweight

ave (āv)

1

brave
cave
crave
Dave
gave
grave
knave
pave

rave
save
shave
slave
wave
(waive)

2

behave
deprave
engrave
enslave
forgave

aved (āvd)

1

braved
caved
craved
paved
raved
saved
shaved
slaved
waved
(waived)

2

behaved
engraved
enslaved
repaved

aze (āz)

1

blaze
braise
(braze)
craze
daze
faze
(phase)
gaze
glaze
graze

haze
laze
maze
(maize)
phrase
praise
raise
(raze)
vase
ways

2 ———————

ablaze
amaze
appraise
deglaze
rephrase

sideways
upraise

3 ———————

hollandaise
mayonnaise
nowadays
one-act plays
paraphrase
reappraise

azed (āzd)

1 ———————

blazed
braised
crazed
dazed

fazed
gazed
glazed
grazed
hazed
lazed
phased
phrased
praised
raised
(razed)

2 ———————

amazed
appraised
deglazed

rephrased
upraised

3 ———————

paraphrased
reappraised

Double ay (ā) sounds

Love is the greatest thing,
The oldest, yet the latest thing.

—*"Love Is the Greatest Thing,"* words and music by
Ray Noble

ayber
(āb′ər)

2
labor
neighbor
saber
tabor

ayby (āb′ē)

2
baby
maybe

able (āb′əl)

2
able
cable
fable
gable
label
Mabel
stable
table

3
enable
unable
timetable
turntable
unstable

abled
(āb′əld)

2
cabled
fabled
gabled
labeled
stabled
tabled

abler
(āb′lər)

2
abler
cabler
fabler
labeler
stabler

abling
(āb′lĭng)

2
cabling
labeling
stabling
tabling

ayday
(ād′ā)

2
heyday
Mayday
payday

aded
(ād′ĭd)

2
aided
bladed
raided
traded
faded
gladed
braided
shaded
jaded
spaded
graded
waded

3
unaided
unbraided
brocaded
invaded
persuaded
degraded
cascaded

unfaded
dissuaded
evaded
pervaded
blockaded
paraded
crusaded

ader (ād′ər)

2
aider
braider
seder
grader
staider
raider
trader
wader

3
unbraider
invader
upbraider
dissuader
crusader
persuader
parader

ady (ād′ē)

2
Grady
shady

11

lady
Brady
Sadie
'fraidy

3
milady
fore-lady
O'Grady

**ading
(ād'ĭng)**

2
aiding
spading
grading
fading
raiding
trading
lading
braiding
shading

3
wading
unfading
degrading
invading
blockading
parading
crusading
pervading
persuading
cascading
unbraiding
evading
dissuading

**aidless
(ād'lĭs)**

2
aidless
spadeless
tradeless

braidless
shadeless
bladeless
gradeless

ayer (ā'ər)

2
gayer
player
payer
prayer
(preyer)
strayer
layer
slayer
brayer
sprayer
weigher
flayer
mayor
grayer
stayer
obeyer

3
waylayer
outlayer
forayer
betrayer
soothsayer
purveyor
delayer
displayer
hoorayer
portrayer
inveigher
bricklayer
taxpayer
defrayer
essayer
conveyer
surveyor

**aying
(ā'ĭng)**

2
baying
neighing
praying
(preying)
weighing
laying
fraying
straying
slaying
(sleighing)
graying
saying

3
croqueting
obeying
displaying
decaying
portraying
conveying
waylaying
dismaying
essaying
surveying
parleying
defraying
crocheting
reweighing
prepaying

ages (āj'ĭz)

2
ages
pages
stages
gauges
rages
wages
cages
sages

3
encages
engages
outrages
presages

**aging
(āj'ĭng)**

2
aging
paging
gauging
raging
caging
waging
staging

**ageless
(āj'lĭs)**

2
ageless
pageless
gaugeless
stageless
cageless
wageless

**ageous
(āj'əs)**

3
rampageous
contagious
outrageous
enrageous
courageous

akin (āk'ĭn)

2
Aiken
shaken

bacon
taken
Macon
waken

3
Jamaican
mistaken
wind-shaken
forsaken
awaken
unshaken
untaken

aker (āk′ər)

2
acre
(acher)
laker
breaker
staker
baker
maker
slaker
shaker
waker
faker
raker
taker
Quaker

3
wiseacre
bookmaker
lawmaker
heartbreaker
saltshaker
matchmaker
peacemaker
shoemaker
lawbreaker
partaker
painstaker
watchmaker

dressmaker
strikebreaker
forsaker
mistaker

aking (āk′ĭng)

2
aching
raking
waking
baking
braking
(breaking)
faking
shaking
taking
quaking
slaking

3
watchmaking
heartbreaking
mistaking
bookmaking
forsaking
dressmaking
partaking
painstaking

aikless (āk′lĭs)

2
acheless
rakeless
stakeless
(steakless)
fakeless
breakless
wakeless
snakeless
takeless
quakeless

ailant (āl′ənt)

3
inhalant
exhalant
surveillant
assailant

ailer (āl′ər)

2
baler
(bailer)
mailer
frailer
sailor
staler
jailer
nailer
trailer
tailor
(Taylor)
scaler
paler
wailer
(whaler)

3
regaler
assailer
inhaler
wholesaler
exhaler
retailer

ailess (āl′ĭs)

2
dayless
rayless
prayless
(preyless)
swayless

payless
wayless

ailest (āl′ĭst)

2
palest
frailest
stalest

aily (āl′ē)

2
Bailey
snaily
daily
waily
gaily
Yalie

ailing (āl′ĭng)

2
ailing
hailing
mailing
nailing
trailing
veiling
jailing
paling
sailing
failing
flailing
scaling
railing
tailing
wailing
(whaling)

3
unfailing
exhaling
wholesaling

entailing
unveiling
availing
regaling
blackmailing
detailing
curtailing
inhaling
impaling
retailing
dovetailing
prevailing

4 —————
unavailing

**aimer
(ām′ər)**

2 —————
aimer
blamer
namer
gamer
claimer
framer
tamer
lamer
maimer
shamer

3 —————
acclaimer
disclaimer
reclaimer
exclaimer
proclaimer
nicknamer

**aimful
(ām′fəl)**

2 —————
aimful
gameful
shameful
blameful

amy (ām′ē)

2 —————
Amy
flamy
gamy
Jamie
Mamie

**aiming
(ām′ĭng)**

2 —————
aiming
blaming
maiming
shaming
gaming
flaming
naming
laming
claiming
framing
taming

3 —————
acclaiming
disclaiming
nicknaming
reclaiming
declaiming
exclaiming
proclaiming
inflaming
misnaming

**aimless
(ām′lĭs)**

2 —————
aimless
blameless
nameless
fameless
claimless
shameless

gameless
flameless
tameless

**ainful
(ān′fəl)**

2 —————
baneful
gainful
painful

3 —————
disdainful
ungainful
complainful

**ainy
(ān′ē)**

2 —————
Janey
grainy
rainy
veiny
brainy
zany

4 —————
Allegheny
miscellany

**ainger
(ān′jər)**

2 —————
changer
ranger
danger
stranger
manger

3 —————
exchanger
endanger
shortchanger

deranger
arranger

**ainging
(ān′jĭng)**

2 —————
changing
ranging

3 —————
exchanging
shortchanging
unchanging
deranging
estranging

**ainless
(ān′lĭs)**

2 —————
chainless
painless
grainless
gainless
rainless
stainless
strainless
maneless
brainless
vaneless
(veinless)

**ainly
(ān′lē)**

2 —————
plainly
vainly
mainly
sanely

3 —————
urbanely
profanely
insanely
humanely

14

ainment
(ān′mənt)

3
enchainment
arraignment
ordainment
attainment
retainment
regainment
detainment

aping
(āp′ĭng)

2
aping
scraping
gaping
shaping
draping
taping

3
escaping
reshaping
landscaping
skyscraping
retaping

airest
(ār′ĭst)

2
barest
fairest
rarest

airful
(ār′fəl)

2
dareful
careful
prayerful

airy (ār′ē)

2
airy
Gary
scary
prairie
wary
dairy
hairy
Mary
fairy
Carey
snary
vary

3
contrary
rosemary
unwary
canary

airing
(ār′ĭng)

2
airing
faring
scaring
glaring
sharing
swearing
wearing
bearing
caring
blaring
pairing
(paring)
tearing
daring
chairing
flaring
sparing
staring
snaring

3
seafaring
impairing
outwearing
declaring
despairing
outswearing
repairing
outstaring
forswearing

airless
(ār′lĭs)

2
airless
chairless
pairless
shareless
heirless
hairless
glareless
spareless
careless
snareless
prayerless
stairless

airly (ār′lē)

2
barely
fairly
squarely
rarely

airness
(ār′nĭs)

2
bareness
rareness
fairness
thereness
whereness
spareness
squareness

acer (ās′ər)

2
acer
caser
pacer
bracer
chaser
lacer
placer
spacer
baser
tracer
facer
macer
racer

3
eraser
disgracer
grimacer
horse racer
retracer
replacer
displacer
embracer
encaser
misplacer

aishul
(āsh′əl)

2
facial
glacial
racial
spatial

aishun
(āsh′ən)

2
nation
ration
station

3

probation
vocation
creation
relation
inflation
summation
donation
vibration
migration
filtration
cessation
dictation
potation
substation
mutation
starvation
vexation
vacation
gradation
ligation
elation
deflation
collation
formation
cognation
phonation
hydration
oration
duration
causation
plantation
flotation
rotation
gestation
fixation
location
foundation
oblation
gelation
cremation
planation
damnation
pronation
serration

nitration
gyration
pulsation
dentation
notation
quotation
flirtation
crustacean
ovation
taxation

aishus
(āsh′əs)

2

spacious
gracious

3

sebaceous
fallacious
veracious
herbaceous
tenacious
ungracious
flirtatious
audacious
capacious
loqvacious
curvaceous
bodacious

acing
(ās′ĭng)

2

acing
casing
spacing
chasing
lacing
racing
tracing
facing

pacing
bracing
placing

3

debasing
encasing
misplacing
grimacing
effacing
horse racing
displacing
disgracing
defacing
replacing
embracing
erasing
unlacing

aceless
(ās′lĭs)

2

aceless
caseless
maceless
raceless
traceless
baseless
laceless
paceless
graceless
faceless
placeless
spaceless
braceless
vaseless

asted
(ās′tĭd)

2

basted
tasted

hasted
wasted
(waisted)
pasted

ated (āt′ĭd)

2

bated
(baited)
gated
(gaited)
rated
stated
dated
hated
grated
waited
(weighted)
fated
mated
sated
crated

3

abated
predated
created
belated
inflated
cremated
instated
debated
postdated
ill-fated
related
checkmated
berated
rebated
outdated
elated
deflated
stalemated
frustrated
awaited
unmated

ater (āt'ər)

2

cater
later
crater
stater
dater
slater
gaiter
greater
(grater)
satyr
(sater)
skater
pater
traitor
waiter

3

probator
creator
debater
collator
donator
gyrator
dictator
mandator
legator
translator
vibrator
narrator
pulsator
locator
negator
relator
cremator
migrator
curator
spectator
equator

4

elevator
navigator

aviator
alligator
instigator
regulator
delegator
violator
fumigator

aty (āt'ē)

2

eighty
Leyte
Haiti
Katie
weighty
matey

aytime (āt'īm)

2

daytime
May time
pay time
play time

ating (āt'ĭng)

2

baiting
skating
rating
sating
dating
slating
stating
grating
hating
mating
crating
waiting
(weighting)

3

abating
relating
debating
inflating
postdating
awaiting

aitless (āt'lĭs)

3

baitless
gateless
traitless
dateless
hateless
freightless
weightless
fateless
mateless
grateless
stateless

aitly (āt'lē)

2

lately
greatly
stately
straightly

aven (āv'ən)

2

haven
craven
raven
maven
graven
shaven

aver (āv'ər)

2

favor
flavor
raver
craver
waver
(waiver)
slaver
braver
saver
(savor)
paver
graver
shaver
quaver

3

disfavor
depraver
enslaver
lifesaver
engraver
timesaver

avy (āv'ē)

2

Davy
gravy
wavy
navy

aving (āv'ĭng)

2

paving
craving
waving
(waiving)
raving
saving
braving
shaving
slaving

3

behaving
engraving
depraving
timesaving
enslaving
lifesaving

azen
(āz′ən)

2

brazen
raisin

azer (āz′ər)

2

gazer
mazer
grazer
hazer
raiser
(razor)
(razer)

blazer
phraser
praiser

3

stargazer
upraiser
appraiser

Triple ay (ā) sounds

Embrace me, my sweet embraceable you,
Embrace me, you irreplaceable you!

—*"Embraceable You," lyric by Ira Gershwin, music by*
George Gershwin

ayable
(ā′əbəl)

3 —————
playable
weighable
payable
sayable
swayable
flayable

aikable
(āk′əbəl)

3 —————
acheable
breakable
takable
shakeable
makeable
fakeable

aikery
(āk′ərē)

3 —————
bakery
fakery
Quakery
snakery

ailable
(āl′əbəl)

3 —————
bailable
mailable
salable
(sailable)

4 —————
unsalable
(unsailable)
available
retailable

aimable
(ām′əbəl)

3 —————
aimable
blamable
framable
claimable
namable
tamable

ainable
(ān′əbəl)

3 —————
gainable
drainable

chainable
sprainable
stainable
strainable
planable
trainable

ainfully
(ān′fəlē)

3 —————
banefully
gainfully
painfully

apable
(āp′əbəl)

3 —————
capable
drapable
shapable

airable
(ār′əbəl)

3 —————
sparable

bearable
sharable
pairable
tearable
swearable
wearable

airiest
(ār′ēĭst)

3 —————
airiest
hairiest
wariest
glariest
chariest

airingly
(ār′ĭnglē)

3 —————
daringly
flaringly
sparingly
glaringly

19

aishully
(āsh'əlē)

3 ───────
facially
glacially
racially

aitfully
(āt'fəlē)

3 ───────
fatefully
hatefully
gratefully

slavery
wavery
savory
knavery
quavery

flavoring
savoring
quavering

aishunless
(āsh'ənlĭs)

3 ───────
nationless
rationless
stationless

avery
(āv'ərē)

3 ───────
Avery
bravery

avering
(āv'ərĭng)

3 ───────
favoring
wavering

Single ah (ä) sounds

Oh, Gigi, while you were trembling on the brink,
Was I out yonder somewhere blinking at a star?
Oh, Gigi, have I been standing up too close or back
*   too far?*

—*"Gigi," lyric by Alan Jay Lerner, music by Frederick*
*   Loewe*

ah (ä)

1
blah
bra
ha
la
ma
pa
rah
spa

2
Grandma
Grandpa
hurrah
Mama
Papa

3
Bogotá
Panama

ahd (äd)

1
quad
wad

2
façade
glissade
hurrahed

ahzh (äzh)

2
barrage
corsage
garage
massage
mirage

ahk (äk)

1
jock
lock
block
flock
clock
smock
knock
rock
sock
shock
cock
hock

2
woodcock
peacock
Bangkok
wedlock

padlock
shylock
hemlock
unlock
bedrock
tick-tock
restock
livestock

3
Antioch
stumbling
   block
interlock
Little Rock
laughing
   stock
overstock

ahks (äks)

1
ox
box
fox
pox
lox

2
sandbox
strongbox

jukebox
mailbox
pillbox
hatbox
smallpox
ham hocks

3
chatterbox
paradox
orthodox
Goldilocks
chicken pox

ahl (äl)

2
chorale
locale
morale

3
admiral
aerial
animal
biblical
capital
carnival
casual
cerebral
classical
comical

21

cynical
digital
ethical
hospital
interval
magical
marital
medical
mineral
minimal
musical
mystical
mythical
nautical
optical
orbital
physical
principal
punctual
radial
radical
regional
seasonal
serial
several
sexual
skeletal
Taj Mahal
technical
topical
typical
usual
vertebral
vertical
virtual
visual
whimsical

ahlv (älv)

2 ———————
absolve
resolve
dissolve
evolve

revolve
involve

ahm (äm)

1 ———————
calm
Guam
palm
psalm
Dom
mom
prom
Tom
qualm

ahmp (ämp)

1 ———————
comp
pomp
romp
stomp
swamp

ahn (än)

2 ———————
Iran
Koran
pecan
hereon
thereon
bonbon
chiffon
Yukon
salon
Ceylon
upon
Tucson
baton
(Bataan)
Yvonne

3 ———————
Audubon
mastodon

octagon
pentagon
hexagon
Oregon
undergone
leprechaun
Little John
silicon
Avalon
echelon
Babylon
Parthenon
hereupon
thereupon
whereupon
Oberon
Amazon
Barbizon
liaison

ahnd (änd)

1 ———————
bond
fond
blond
pond
spawned
wand

2 ———————
abscond
respond
beyond
despond

ahp (äp)

1 ———————
bop
chop
hop
cop
flop

plop
slop
mop
pop
drop
crop
prop
shop
top
stop
swap
fop

2 ———————
raindrop
teardrop
dewdrop
eavesdrop
workshop
pawnshop
tip-top
backstop
nonstop
shortstop
flip-flop

3 ———————
soda pop
lollipop
whistle stop

ahped (äpt)

1 ———————
chopped
hopped
flopped
plopped
slopped
mopped
popped
dropped
stopped
cropped
topped
propped

ar (är)

1

are
bar
car
czar
far
mar
jar
par
scar
spar
star
tar

2

afar
ajar
bazaar
(bizarre)
cigar
crossbar
crowbar
guitar
polestar
sidecar
streetcar
sitar
savoir

3

Bolivar
caviar
evening star
jaguar
railroad car
repertoire
Zanzibar

arch (ärch)

1

arch
march
larch

parch
starch

ard (ärd)

1

bard
(barred)
card
charred
guard
hard
jarred
marred
lard
scarred
sparred
tarred
yard

2

back yard
barnyard
Bernard
bombard
courtyard
discard
Gerard
lifeguard
regard
retard
safeguard
stockyard

3

avant-garde
bodyguard
boulevard
disregard

arge (ärj)

1

barge
charge
large
Marge
sarge

2

discharge
enlarge
surcharge
at large

ark (ärk)

1

arc
(ark)
bark
Clark
dark
hark
lark
narc
mark
park
shark
spark
stark

2

birthmark
Denmark
earmark
embark
hallmark
landmark
monarch
Ozark
postmark
remark
skylark
bulwark

3

disembark
watermark

arked (ärkt)

1

arced
barked

harked
marked
parked
sparked

3

disembarked
watermarked

arm (ärm)

1

arm
charm
farm
harm

2

alarm
disarm
firearm
forearm
schoolmarm
yardarm

arn (ärn)

1

barn
darn
yarn

arp (ärp)

1

carp
harp
sharp
tarp

art (ärt)

1

art
dart
mart
tart
Bart

23

hart
(heart)
smart
chart
cart
part
start

2 ———————
sweetheart
go-cart
faintheart
apart
impart
redstart
upstart
dogcart
depart
rampart
re-start

3 ———————
à la carte
sugar tart
counterpart
apple tart

ahsh (äsh)

1 ———————
gosh
josh
posh
slosh
wash
quash
squash

2 ———————
galosh
rewash
eyewash
hogwash
backwash
wish-wash
whitewash

aht (ät)

1 ———————
what
(watt)

squat
swat
yacht
lot
blot
plot
slot
knot
(not)
pot
spot
shot

2 ———————
Cabot
abbot
robot
begot
forgot
cannot
whatnot
slingshot
buckshot
gunshot

snapshot
upshot
earshot
grapeshot

3 ———————
apricot
patriot
Lancelot
counterplot
Huguenot
argonaut
juggernaut
flowerpot
coffeepot
overshot

Double ah (ä) sounds

Fredrick: She flutters. Desiree: How charming.
Fredrick: She twitters. Desiree: My word!
Fredrick: She floats. Desiree: Isn't that alarming?
  What is she, a bird?

—*"You Must Meet My Wife," words and music by*
  Stephen Sondheim

ahber
(äb′ər)

2
jobber
slobber
robber
sobber

ahby (äb′ē)

2
Bobby
hobby
lobby
snobby

ahbing
(äb′ing)

2
bobbing
jobbing
lobbing
mobbing
snobbing
robbing
throbbing
sobbing

ahble
(äb′əl)

2
gobble
cobble

wobble
squabble
bobble
nobble

ahbler
(äb′lər)

2
gobbler
hobbler
cobbler
wobbler
squabbler

ahbling
(äb′ling)

2
hobbling
wobbling
squabbling
cobbling
gobbling

ahching
(äch′ing)

2
blotching
notching
watching

ahda (äd′ə)

3
colada
Grenada
armada
Nevada
Granada

ahded
(äd′əd)

2
plodded
prodded
sodded
wadded
nodded

ahder
(äd′ər)

2
odder
fodder
nodder
plodder
solder

ahdy (äd′ē)

2
body
shoddy
toddy

3
somebody
nobody

ahdik
(äd′ĭk)

3
melodic
spasmodic

ahgger
(äg′ər)

2
jogger
logger
(lager)
flogger

ahgging
(äg′ing)

2
jogging
logging
flogging
hogging
slogging
bogging

ahket
(äk′ĭt)

2
docket
locket

pocket
rocket
crocket
sprocket
socket

3 ———————
pickpocket
hip pocket
air pocket
skyrocket

**ahky
(äk′ē)**

2 ———————
hockey
jockey
rocky
stocky

**ahking
(äk′ĭng)**

2 ———————
docking
clocking
mocking
knocking
rocking
crocking
shocking
stocking
locking
blocking

ahla (äl′ə)

2 ———————
Allah
gala
wallah
challah

3 ———————
koala
impala
Marsala

ahler (äl′ər)

2 ———————
dollar
collar
scholar
holler
Mahler

**ahledge
(äl′ĭj)**

2 ———————
college
knowledge

ahly (äl′ē)

2 ———————
dolly
holly
jolly
collie
Molly
Polly
volley
trolley
folly

2 ———————
Ali
Bali

3 ———————
Bengali
Somali
tamale
finale

**ahlo
(äl′ō)**

2 ———————
follow
hollow

wallow
swallow
Rollo

**ahma
(äm′ə)**

2 ———————
mama
Brahma
llama
drama
Rama
grama

3 ———————
Bahama
pajama

**ahmis
(äm′ĭs)**

2 ———————
promise
Thomas

ahna (än′ə)

3 ———————
Guiana
nirvana
mañana
sultana
iguana

**ahnded
(än′dĭd)**

3 ———————
unbonded
absconded
responded

**ahnder
(än′dər)**

2 ———————
ponder
wander
squander
yonder
fonder

**ahnik
(än′ĭk)**

2 ———————
tonic
chronic
phonic
sonic

3 ———————
carbonic
bubonic
sardonic
symphonic
ionic
harmonic
ironic
platonic

**ahper
(äp′ər)**

2 ———————
chopper
copper
cropper
proper
shopper
topper
swapper
whopper
dropper
popper
stopper
mopper

3
grasshopper
eavesdropper
improper

**ahpik
(ăp′ĭk)**

2
tropic
topic

**ahping
(ăp′ĭng)**

2
chopping
flopping
clopping
mopping
dropping
shopping
stopping
topping
swapping
popping
whopping
propping

3
eavesdropping
clodhopping
clip-clopping

**ahrded
(är′dĭd)**

2
larded
carded
guarded

3
bombarded
discarded
safeguarded
regarded

placarded
retarded

argo (är′gō)

2
Argo
largo
Fargo
Margo
cargo

**arker
(är′kər)**

2
barker
larker
sparker
darker
marker
harker
parker
starker

**arless
(är′lĭs)**

2
barless
jarless
starless
carless
scarless
tarless
czarless

**arling
(är′lĭng)**

2
darling
gnarling
snarling
marling
starling

**arming
(är′mĭng)**

2
arming
harming
charming
farming

3
alarming
uncharming
forearming
disarming

**arnished
(är′nĭsht)**

2
garnished
tarnished
varnished

**arson
(är′sən)**

2
arson
Carson
parson

**arted
(är′tĭd)**

2
darted
charted
hearted
smarted
started
carted
parted

3
kindhearted
weakhearted
softhearted

stouthearted
outsmarted
hardhearted
warmhearted
lighthearted
truehearted
departed
upstarted
freehearted
downhearted
fainthearted
uncharted
imparted

**arter
(är′tər)**

2
barter
garter
smarter
charter
carter
tartar
darter
martyr
starter

**arting
(är′tĭng)**

2
charting
smarting
darting
parting
carting
starting

3
sweethearting
restarting
departing
self-starting
imparting
upstarting

**ahshing
(äsh′ĭng)**

2

washing
joshing
squashing

**ahted
(ät′əd)**

2

dotted
jotted
blotted
clotted
plotted
knotted
rotted
potted
spotted

trotted
swatted

**ahten
(ät′ən)**

3

gotten
rotten

3

begotten
ill-gotten
forgotten

ahter (ät′ər)

2

otter
hotter
jotter
blotter
plotter

spotter
totter
trotter
water
squatter
swatter
yachter
potter

**ahting
(ät′ĭng)**

2

dotting
jotting
blotting
clotting
plotting
potting
spotting
trotting

yachting
rotting
knotting

**ahtless
(ät′lĭs)**

2

dotless
blotless
plotless
potless
spotless

ahto (ät′ō)

2

Otto
motto
grotto
lotto

28

Single a (ă) sounds

So prepare, say a pray'r
Send the word, send the word over there.

—"Over There," words and music by George M. Cohan

ab (ăb)

1
dab
scab
slab
grab
gab
lab
crab
stab
cab
blab
drab
tab
fab

3
baobab
taxicab

atch (ăch)

1
batch
latch
patch
hatch
match
scratch
catch
snatch
thatch
natch

2
nuthatch
dispatch
attach
mismatch
detach
unlatch
repatch
kneepatch

atched (ăcht)

1
batched
matched
scratched
hatched
snatched
thatched
latched
patched

2
mismatched
dispatched
detached
attached
unmatched

ad (ăd)

1
ad
(add)

dad
had
lad
clad
pad
sad
fad
cad
plaid
brad
bad
gad
Chad
glad
mad
grad
tad

2
readd
egad
Sinbad
forbad
unclad

3
Iliad
iron-clad
ivy-clad
myriad
winter-clad
Leningrad
Trinidad
heavy-clad
undergrad

aff (ăf)

1
laugh
gaff
graph
calf
staff

2
behalf
carafe
flagstaff
mooncalf
riffraff
horselaugh
giraffe
distaff
Falstaff

3
phonograph
autograph
epitaph
paragraph
monograph
bellylaugh
photograph

better half
telegraph
Dictograph
lithograph
quarterstaff
epigraph
cenotaph

aft (ăft)

1

aft
laughed
graft
Taft
daft
raft
craft
gaffed
draft
shaft
staffed

2

witchcraft
folk craft
woodcraft
aircraft

3

overdraft
handicraft
metalcraft

agg (ăg)

1

bag
scag
nag
brag
sag
wag
fag
lag
snag

drag
shag
swag
gag
flag
rag
scrag
tag
jag

2

handbag
wigwag
zigzag

3

moneybag
saddlebag
scalawag
luggage tag

ack (ăk)

1

back
lack
plaque
smack
pack
(pac)
track
tack
quack
hack
black
slack
flak
knack
rack
sack
(sac)
stack
yak
jack
clack
(claque)

Mack
(mac)
snack
crack
shack
Wac
(whack)

2

way back
switchback
crookback
comeback
humpback
blackjack
skipjack
lampblack
repack
wisecrack
racetrack
attack
thumbtack
holdback
quillback
drawback
horseback
flapjack
shellac
bootblack
unpack
retrack
woolsack
hardtack
haystack
hunchback
halfback
fullback
throwback
kayak
knicknack
woolpack
backtrack
ransack
ticktack
bullwhack

3

zodiac
Pontiac
razorback
bric-a-brac
haversack
cardiac
piggyback
quarterback
Union Jack
tamarack
bivouac
maniac
leatherback
almanac
cul-de-sac
paddywhack
paperback

ax (ăks)

1

ax
lax
(lacks)
Max
packs
sax
(sacks)
wax
(whacks)
backs
flax
tracks
tax
(tacks)
jacks
slacks
snacks
thwacks
stacks
yaks

2

pickax
climax
haystacks
greenbacks
backtracks
relax
ransacks
beeswax

3

battle-ax
Halifax
overtax
parallax
income tax
jumping jacks

akt (ăkt)

1

act
pact
(packed)
tract
(tracked)
fact
racked
(wracked)
tact
(tacked)
whacked
lacked
cracked
quacked

2

react
enact
unpacked
sidetracked
intact
hunchbacked
impact
ransacked
contact
contract

hump-backed
compact
entr'acte
transact
exact

3

counteract
cataract
overact
interact
re-enact
inexact

al (ăl)

1

Al
pal
gal
Sal
Cal
shall
Hal

2

locale
morale
canal
corral
(chorale)
La Salle

3

musicale
chaparral
pastorale

am (ăm)

1

am
ham
lam
(lamb)
slam
ram
tram

swam
bam
jam
clam
ma'am
gram
Sam
tam
wham
dam
(damn)
cam
flam
Pam
cram
sham
yam

2

madame
Siam
Assam
beldam
Khayyam
grandam
flimflam
whimwham

3

Alabam'
Nottingham
telegram
centigram
Abraham
diaphragm
milligram
cablegram
monogram
Uncle Sam
Birmingham
anagram
epigram
kilogram
cryptogram
Amsterdam

amp (ămp)

1

amp
camp
lamp
tramp
champ
scamp
ramp
stamp
damp
clamp
cramp
vamp

2

encamp
revamp
unclamp

an (ăn)

1

Ann
tan
Dan
clan
pan
ran
ban
can
plan
Pan
bran
Chan
fan
scan
man
span
Fran
Stan
van
flan

2

sedan	schoolman	capman	cowman
cancan	pecan	tipman	caiman
madman	Milan	barman	wayman
clubman	cabman	German	hardpan
headman	sandman	merman	trepan
odd man	birdman	floorman	inspan
iceman	lineman	leadsman	outran
bargeman	wireman	landsman	gratin
capstan	Norseman	guardsman	sampan
shoreman	yeggman	tribesman	outspan
flagman	tugman	salesman	Bataan
swagman	ranchman	statesman	Chopin
hangman	churchman	marksman	Iran
coachman	freshman	groomsman	rattan
henchman	wise man	townsman	divan
watchman	bankman	batsman	
Dutchman	oilman	yachtsman	**3**
Welshman	millman	sportsman	also-ran
Pac-Man	Pullman	boatman	Peter Pan
stockman	trainman	postman	Marianne
bookman	gunman	bowman	African
bellman	woman	plowman	Oppidan
dolman	shipman	playman	Michigan
began	topman	Saipan	lesbian
ashcan	spearman	Roman	guardian
seaman	Sherman	chapman	ruffian
subman	Norman	shopman	Pythian
leadman	headman	carman	thespian
bandman	Batman	Herman	Chinaman
fireman	woodsman	airman	Orangeman
brakeman	swordsman	beadsman	rifleman
freeman	spokesman	bedpan	signalman
horseman	helmsman	bondsman	alderman
ragman	kinsman	herdsman	waterman
game plan	pressman	tradesman	sailorman
songman	draftsman	trash can	talisman
Frenchman	Scotsman	dragsman	selectman
switchman	meatman	bailsman	clergyman
ploughman	footman	clansman	Caliban
Bushman	crewman	oarsman	Vatican
milkman	showman	craftsman	suffragan
workman	layman	huntsman	Mulligan
billman	Japan	CAT-scan	Jonathan
tollman	yoeman	pitman	Nubian
	shaman	Truman	Gordian

Fijian
Julian
husbandman
nobleman
gentleman
dragoman
fisherman
slaughterman
backwoodsman
frontiersman
merchantman
tallyman
Caliban
Mexican
cardigan
hooligan
Serbian
Indian
Lydian
Georgian
Anglican
Caspian
Austrian
policeman
middleman
longshoreman
midshipman
superman
quarterman
Irishman
highwayman
liveryman
dairyman
countryman
Parmesan
Pakistan
Libyan
ferryman
Lutheran
courtesan
Puritan
caravan
merryman
Yucatan
Turkestan

cordovan
Wesleyan

and (ănd)

1

and
fanned
scanned
gland
panned
grand
tanned
band
hand
land
planned
spanned
strand
banned
canned
bland
manned
brand
sand
stand

2

headband
breastband
backhand
firsthand
woodland
Greenland
lowland
moorland
wasteland
remand
quicksand
neckband
wristband
unhand
headland
mainland
Rhineland
Lapland

grassland
northland
command
lampstand
disband
offhand
shorthand
midland
dreamland
inland
upland
Queensland
demand
expand
withstand
left-hand
right-hand

3

contraband
overhand
wonderland
motherland
countermand
four-in-hand
underhand
upper hand
borderland
overland
Rio Grande
secondhand
fairyland
fatherland
reprimand
understand
ampersand

ang (ăng)

1

bang
hang
slang
sang
fang
pang

swang
whang
gang
clang
sprang
twang
rang

ank (ănk)

1

dank
blank
plank
frank
(franc)
crank
shank
swank
bank
hank
flank
spank
prank
tank
lank
clank
rank
sank
thank
yank

2

embank
gangplank
redshank
pointblank
foreshank
outflank
outrank
handcrank

3

mountebank
riverbank
savings bank
antitank

ance (ănts)

1

chance
glance
trance
dance
France
lance
prance
stance

2

séance
finance
brilliance
perchance
enhance
askance
expanse
advance
mischance
romance
entrance
semblance

3

disturbance
ascendance
arrogance
nonchalance
ambulance
countenance
ordinance
consonance
governance
sufferance
temperance
ignorance
circumstance
misguidance
radiance
jubilance
sustenance
dominance
assonance
remembrance

furtherance
utterance
aberrance
repentance
avoidance
elegance
variance
vigilance
maintenance
convenance
resonance
dissonance
encumbrance
tolerance
severance
acceptance
clairvoyance

anced (ănst)

1

chanced
glanced
danced
lanced
pranced

2

enhanced
entranced
romanced
financed
advanced

ant (ănt)

1

ant
(aunt)
scant
pant
shan't
chant
plant
rant
can't

(cant)
slant
grant

2

enchant
replant
transplant
courante
decant
descant
eggplant
supplant
gallant
houseplant
implant
aslant

3

radiant
mendicant
confidant
congregant
litigant
elephant
revelant
stimulant
informant
dominant
dissonant
ignorant
irritant
debutante
applicant
lubricant
triumphant
jubilant
covenant
consonant
celebrant
emigrant
habitant
hesitant
issuant
toxicant
elegant

irrigant
arrogant
nonchalant
vigilant
postulant
assonant
tolerant
immigrant
registrant
militant
important

ap (ăp)

1

chap
cap
flap
map
pap
scrap
sap
dap
lap
(Lapp)
clap
nap
(knap)
rap
(wrap)
trap
tap
gap
slap
snap
crap
strap
yap

2

stopgap
madcap
kneecap
uncap
unsnap
whitecap

mantrap
redcap
recap
icecap
flip-flap
roadmap
entrap
mishap
skullcap
nightcap
backslap
unwrap
giftwrap
blackstrap

3
handicap
photomap
overlap
thunderclap
rattletrap
Christmas
    wrap

ass (ăs)

1
ass
lass
mass
grass
bass
glass
pass
crass
gas
class
brass
sass
Tass

2
jackass
Midas
reclass
remass

Thomas
impasse
harass
Kansas
fracas
eyeglass
spyglass
first class
world class
outclass
Christmas
surpass
Madras
crevasse
hourglass
amass
en masse
compass
trespass
terrace
Texas

3
contrabass
looking glass
working class
super-class
Pythias
Candlemas
Khyber Pass
coup-de-grace
pancreas
weatherglass
underclass
bonny lass
alias
underpass
middle-class
upper-class
Nicholas
Elias
overpass
sassafrass

ash (ăsh)

1
ash
gash
lash
splash
smash
crash
bash
hash
flash
slash
rash
thrash
stash
dash
cash
clash
mash
brash
sash

2
abash
backlash
rehash
eyelash
mustache

ashed (ăsht)

1
bashed
hashed
flashed
slashed
crashed
dashed
cashed
clashed
mashed
thrashed
stashed
gashed

lashed
splashed
smashed
sashed

2
abashed
rehashed
mustached

ask (ăsk)

1
ask
flask
bask
mask
cask
task

asp (ăsp)

1
asp
clasp
gasp
rasp
hasp
grasp

ast (ăst)

1
fast
last
past
(passed)
gassed
blast
vast
cast
(caste)
mast
(massed)

2
bombast
downcast

35

outcast
ballast
amassed
dynast
harassed
broadcast
steadfast
breakfast
outlast
mainmast
repast
(repassed)
contrast
forecast
miscast
hold fast
aghast
outclassed
gymnast
surpassed

3 ⎯⎯⎯⎯⎯⎯
unsurpassed
overcast

counterblast
flabbergast

at (ăt)

1 ⎯⎯⎯⎯⎯⎯
at
fat
scat
slat
pat
brat
prat
that
bat
hat
flat
mat
(matte)
spat
drat
sprat
chat

cat
splat
gnat
rat
frat
sat
vat

2 ⎯⎯⎯⎯⎯⎯
hereat
thereat
top hat
wildcat
chitchat
hellcat
bearcat
whereat
bobcat
polecat

3 ⎯⎯⎯⎯⎯⎯
acrobat
pussy cat
pitapat
democrat

plutocrat
tabby cat
lariat
bureaucrat
kitty cat
diplomat
Ararat
autocrat
thermostat
automat
baseball bat

ath (ăth)

1 ⎯⎯⎯⎯⎯⎯
bath
lath
path
math
wrath

2 ⎯⎯⎯⎯⎯⎯
bypath
warpath
footpath

Double a (ă) sounds

The smallest Malay rabbit,
Deplores this stupid habit.

—*"Mad Dogs and Englishmen," words and music by*
Noel Coward

abby (ăb′ē)

2
abbey
(Abbie)
cabby
crabby
scabby
shabby
gabby
flabby
blabby
tabby

abit (ăb′ĭt)

2
Babbitt
habit
rabbet
(rabbit)

abble (ăb′əl)

2
babble
rabble
dabble
drabble
scrabble
gabble
grabble

atcher (ăch′ər)

2
latcher
patcher
hatcher
matcher
scratcher
catcher
snatcher
thatcher

3
dogcatcher
flycatcher
back scratcher
dispatcher

atches (ăch′əz)

2
batches
latches
hatches
Natchez
matches
catches
patches

3
mismatches
dispatches

detaches
attaches

atching (ăch′ĭng)

2
latching
patching
hatching
matching
scratching
catching
snatching
thatching

3
dispatching
attaching
rematching
detaching
mismatching
back scratch-
ing

atchless (ăch′lĭs)

2
latchless
scratchless
hatchless

matchless
catchless
patchless
thatchless

adder (ăd′ər)

2
bladder
gadder
gladder
sadder
ladder
madder
adder

addy (ăd′ē)

2
daddy
caddy
(caddie)
laddie
paddy

addle (ăd′əl)

2
paddle
addle

37

raddle
saddle
straddle

addled
(ăd′əld)

2
paddled
raddled
saddled
straddled
addled

adly (ăd′lē)

2
badly
gladly
sadly
madly

affle (ăf′əl)

2
baffle
raffle
snaffle

after
(ăf′tər)

2
after
drafter
laughter
rafter
grafter
crafter

3
hereafter
thereafter
whereafter

agger
(ăg′ər)

2
bagger
jagger
snagger
stagger
dagger
flagger
ragger
wagger
gagger
nagger
dragger
swagger

aggy (ăg′ē)

2
baggie
(baggy)
haggy
naggy
braggy
shaggy
faggy
craggy
swaggy
Maggie
raggy
scraggy
waggy

aggle
(ăg′əl)

2
gaggle
straggle
haggle
draggle
waggle

acker
(ăk′ər)

2
backer
blacker
smacker
tracker
stacker
hacker
clacker
packer
sacker
lacquer
slacker
cracker
tacker
whacker

3
firecracker
ransacker
bushwhacker
lipsmacker

acky (ăk′ē)

2
hackie
khaki
quacky
jackie
cracky
wacky
tacky

acking
(ăk′ĭng)

2
backing
clacking
racking
(wracking)
sacking
whacking
lacking

smacking
cracking
tacking
blacking
packing
tracking
quacking
snacking

3
shellacking
unpacking
attacking
ransacking

ackle
(ăk′əl)

2
hackle
crackle
cackle
shackle
quackle
mackle
tackle

3
debacle
barnacle
coracle
spectacle
manacle
miracle
ramshackle
pinnacle
oracle
unshackle
obstacle

akshun
(ăk′shən)

2
action
faction
traction
fraction

3

reaction
refraction
contraction
abstraction
transaction
enaction
diffraction
protraction
distraction
olfaction
compaction
infraction
attraction
extraction
exaction
redaction

axy (ăk′sē)

2

flaxy
Maxie
waxy
taxi

**acted
(ăk′tid)**

3

enacted
defracted
detracted
protracted
extracted
reacted
attracted
retracted
abstracted
transacted
exacted
impacted
subtracted
contracted
distracted
contacted

**active
(ăk′tĭv)**

3

reactive
refractive
subtractive
protractive
inactive
diffractive
detractive
abstractive
extractive
attractive
contractive
distractive

allis (ăl′ĭs)

2

Alice
chalice
palace
malice

aloe (ăl′ō)

2

aloe
callow
shallow
fallow
mallow
hallow
sallow
tallow

**amble
(ăm′bəl)**

2

amble
bramble
gamble

scramble
ramble
shamble

**ambler
(ăm′blər)**

2

ambler
scrambler
gambler
rambler
shambler

**ambling
(ăm′blĭng)**

2

ambling
shambling
gambling
rambling
scrambling

**ambles
(ăm′bəlz)**

2

ambles
brambles
gambles
scrambles
rambles
shambles

**ammer
(ăm′ər)**

2

hammer
clamor
grammar
jammer

slammer
crammer
glamour
rammer
shammer

3

sledgehammer
enamor
windjammer

**ammy
(ăm′ē)**

2

hammy
mammy
jammy
Sammy
Tammy
clammy
chamois
(shammy)

**amming
(ăm′ĭng)**

2

damming
(damning)
slamming
shamming
jamming
ramming
clamming
cramming
whamming

**amper
(ăm′pər)**

2

damper
scamper

tamper
hamper
clamper
stamper
vamper
camper
pamper
tramper

amping
(ăm′pĭng)

2 ──────
damping
clamping
tamping
camping
ramping
stamping
scamping
tramping
vamping

anna (ăn′ə)

2 ──────
Anna
Lana
Hannah
manna

3 ──────
bandana
banana
Havana
hosanna
Diana
sultana
savanna
(Savannah)
Guiana
Montana
Susanna

anded
(ăn′dĭd)

2 ──────
banded
landed
stranded
handed
candid
branded
sanded

3 ──────
disbanded
three-handed
blackhanded
unhanded
light-handed
two-handed
remanded
red-handed
highhanded
forehanded
(four-handed)
neat-handed
right-handed
unlanded
commanded
unbranded
free-handed
backhanded
clean-handed
left-handed
shorthanded
demanded
expanded
one-handed

ander
(ăn′dər)

2 ──────
bander
slander
grander

gander
lander
pander
candor
blander
brander
stander

3 ──────
disbander
left-hander
Icelander
demander
expander
meander
right-hander
inlander
remander
backhander
philander
outlander
commander
withstander
Laplander

andy
(ăn′dē)

2 ──────
Andy
candy
randy
dandy
Mandy
brandy
handy
sandy

anding
(ăn′dĭng)

2 ──────
handing
sanding
landing

stranding
standing

3 ──────
disbanding
demanding
outstanding
unhanding
remanding
expanding
commanding
withstanding

andless
(ănd′lĭs)

2 ──────
bandless
glandless
handless
brandless
sandless
landless

anner
(ăn′ər)

2 ──────
banner
planner
panner
spanner
canner
manner
(manor)
tanner
scanner

angle
(ăng′əl)

2 ──────
angle
mangle
wrangle

bangle
spangle
tangle
dangle
jangle
strangle
wangle

3

quadrangle
pentangle
triangle
entangle
untangle
rectangle

anny (ăn′ē)

2

Annie
canny
granny
Danny
clanny
cranny
Fanny
nanny

anic (ăn′ĭk)

3

organic
volcanic
tympanic
tyrannic
satanic
titanic
cyanic
vulcanic
Hispanic
Koranic
tetanic
mechanic
Germanic

Iranic
uranic
Britannic
botanic

anning (ăn′ĭng)

2

banning
scanning
manning
fanning
clanning
panning
tanning
canning
planning
spanning

anker (ăng′kər)

2

anchor
canker
flanker
cranker
tanker
banker
lanker
clanker
pranker
thanker
hanker
blanker
franker
yanker
rancor

anky (ăng′kē)

2

clanky
swanky

hankie
cranky
lanky
pranky
Yankee

anking (ăng′kĭng)

2

banking
spanking
cranking
blanking
ranking
tanking
yanking
clanking
franking
thanking

ankless (ăngk′lĭs)

2

bankless
flankless
tankless
clankless
crankless
blankless
spankless
prankless
thankless

ancer (ăn′sər)

2

answer
lancer
dancer
glancer
cancer
prancer

3

romancer
entrancer
advancer

ancy (ăn′sē)

2

chancy
prancy
fancy
Nancy

3

vacancy
stagnancy
truancy
brilliancy
pregnancy
vagrancy
tenancy
flagrancy
constancy
buoyancy
unfancy
romancy

anter (ăn′tər)

2

banter
scanter
panter
canter
(cantor)
planter
granter
slanter
grantor
ranter

3

enchanter
decanter

transplanter
supplanter

antic
(ăn'tĭk)

2

antic
mantic
frantic

3

gigantic
Atlantic
romantic
semantic

anting
(ăn'tĭng)

2

chanting
panting
slanting
ranting
planting
granting

3

enchanting
decanting
implanting
supplanting

apper
(ăp'ər)

2

clapper
napper
trapper
dapper
slapper
wrapper

strapper
yapper
flapper
mapper
scrapper
tapper

3

kidnapper
wiretapper
entrapper
unwrapper
backslapper

appy (ăp'ē)

2

chappie
nappy
crappy
happy
snappy
scrappy
sappy
mappy
pappy
yappy

apping
(ăp'ĭng)

2

chapping
lapping
slapping
snapping
trapping
gapping
clapping
mapping
rapping
(wrapping)
strapping
yapping

capping
flapping
napping
scrapping
tapping

apple
(ăp'əl)

2

apple
chapel
scrapple
grapple

arry (ăr'ē)

2

carry
(Carrie)
marry
Barry
nary
Harry
Larry
tarry

arrow (ăr'ō)

2

arrow
harrow
barrow
marrow
sparrow
farrow
narrow
Darrow

asses (ăs'ĭz)

2

asses
glasses

passes
gases
classes
lasses
masses
sasses

3

outclasses
molasses
eyeglasses
amasses
harasses
hourglasses
surpasses

asher
(ăsh'ər)

2

gasher
lasher
splasher
smasher
crasher
basher
hasher
clasher
slasher
rasher
thrasher
dasher
casher
flasher
masher
brasher
stasher

ashes
(ăsh'ĭz)

2

ashes
gashes

lashes
splashes
crashes
bashes
hashes
flashes
smashes
dashes
cashes
clashes
rashes
thrashes

3

abashes
backlashes
rehashes
eyelashes
mustaches

**ashing
(ăsh'ĭng)**

2

bashing
cashing
clashing
dashing
lashing
splashing
crashing
hashing
flashing
mashing

assy (ăs'ē)

2

gassy
glassy
brassy
Cassie
classy
sassy

lassie
chassis

**asket
(ăs'kĭt)**

2

basket
gasket
casket

**asted
(ăs'tĭd)**

2

fasted
lasted
blasted

3

bombasted
outlasted
contrasted
three-masted

**aster
(ăs'tər)**

2

faster
blaster
pastor
caster
(Castor)
plaster
master
vaster

3

broadcaster
scoutmaster
choirmaster
forecaster
taskmaster
bushmaster

disaster
paymaster
schoolmaster
postmaster

**astik
(ăs'tĭk)**

2

plastic
spastic
drastic

3

bombastic
scholastic
monastic
sarcastic
dynastic
elastic
gymnastic
fantastic

**asting
(ăs'tĭng)**

fasting
casting
blasting
lasting

3

bombasting
outlasting
broadcasting
forecasting
contrasting

atted (ăt'ĭd)

2

batted
hatted

matted
spatted
chatted
flatted
ratted
dratted
vatted
fatted
platted
patted
tatted

atty (ăt'ē)

2

batty
Hattie
Mattie
chatty
catty
natty
ratty
fatty
patty

attic (ăt'ĭk)

3

Sabbatic
phosphatic
rheumatic
stigmatic
climatic
chromatic
plasmatic
unstatic
quadratic
ecstatic
emphatic
dramatic
dogmatic
somatic

osmatic
pneumatic
lymphatic
schematic
pragmatic
asthmatic

stomatic
traumatic
fanatic
erratic
aquatic

attle (ăt′əl)

2 ——————

battle
rattle
chattel

brattle
tattle
cattle
prattle
wattle

Triple a (ă) sounds

Your looks are laughable,
Unphotographable.

—"My Funny Valentine," lyric by Lorenz Hart, music
  by Richard Rodgers

atchable
(ăch′əbəl)

3
batchable
latchable
patchable
hatchable
matchable
scratchable
catchable
snatchable
thatchable

ackery
(ăk′ərē)

3
hackery
quackery
knackery
Zachary
Thackeray

akshunal
(ăk′shənəl)

3
factional
tractional
fractional

allying
(ăl′ēĭng)

3
dallying
rallying
tallying
sallying

ammerer
(ăm′ərər)

3
hammerer
clamorer
stammerer

ampering
(ăm′pərĭng)

3
hampering
scampering
tampering
pampering

andable
(ăn′dəbəl)

3
bandable
sandable
handable

mandible
standable

appier
(ăp′ēər)

3
happier
scrappier
nappier
snappier
sappier

appiest
(ăp′ēĭst)

3
happiest
scrappiest
nappiest
sappiest
snappiest

arable
(ăr′əbəl)

3
arable
parable

arrier
(ăr′ēər)

3
barrier
harrier
warier
carrier
farrier

arrying
(ăr′ēĭng)

3
harrying
carrying
tarrying
marrying

ashiest
(ăsh′ēĭst)

3
ashiest
flashiest
splashiest
trashiest

ashunul
(ăsh′ənəl)

3
national
passional
rational

45

atterer
(ăt′ərər)

3 ——————
batterer
flatterer
smatterer

chatterer
clatterer
patterer
scatterer
splatterer
shatterer

attering
(at′ərĭng)

3 ——————
battering
flattering
pattering

chattering
clattering
spattering
scattering
smattering
shattering

Single ee (ē) sounds

You came to me from out of nowhere,
You took my heart and found it free,
Wonderful dreams. Wonderful schemes from nowhere,
Made every hour, sweet as a flower for me.

—"Out of Nowhere," lyric by Edward Heyman, music
by Johnny Green

bee (bē)

1
be
(bee)

2
BB
bribee

3
honeybee
wallaby
bumblebee
Barnaby
Araby

dee (dē)

1
Dee

2
MD
Didi

3
COD
tragedy
perfidy
organdy
Burgundy
rhapsody
jeopardy
Ph.D.
remedy

subsidy
Normandy
melody
custody
chickadee
comedy
tweedledee
parody
Lombardy

fee (fē)

1
fee

2
coffee

3
atrophy
salsify

gee (jē)

1
gee

2
clergy
squeegee
pongee
Gigi

3
prodigy
eulogy

effigy
allergy
refugee
strategy
liturgy
perigee

key (kē)

1
key
ski

2
husky
musky
whiskey

3
garlicky
Cherokee
panicky
master key
finicky

lee (lē)

1
lee
(Leigh)
flee
(flea)
glee

2
Leslie

3
Rosalie
Italy
fleur-de-lis

me (mē)

1
me

2
army
swarmy
smarmy

3
infamy
blasphemy
balsamy
Ptolemy
alchemy
enemy
bonhomie

nee (nē)

1
knee

2
trainee
Pawnee
Shawnee
rainy

49

3

Tiffany
larceny
euphony
colony
gluttony
Romany
villainy
cushiony
barony
muttony
nominee
Tuscany
Germany
tyranny
felony
Antony
Anthony
Saxony

pee (pē)

1

pee

2

cowpea
sweatpea
green pea

3

canopy
escapee
recipe

ree (rē)

1

re
spree
free
tree
Brie
three

2

Marie
carefree

dust-free
debris
germ-free
agree
Grand Prix
unfree
heart-free
degree
laundry
theory

3

Barbary
sugary
salary
notary
Calvary
bribery
archery
prudery
roguery
forgery
mockery
scenery
drapery
sorcery
flattery
wintery
mystery
slavery
reverie
shivery
fancy-free
savagery
cavalry
revelry
boundary
diary
bain-marie
library
rotary
ribaldry
robbery
witchery
referee

bakery
rookery
finery
slippery
nursery
watery
artery
feathery
knavery
thievery
silvery
duty-free
mimicry
chivalry
jewelry
dungaree
chicory
summary
contrary
rosary
husbandry
treachery
thundery
drudgery
trickery
gallery
fernery
chancery
battery
lottery
mastery
heathery
bravery
livery
misery
imagery
disagree
rivalry
masonry
jamboree
hickory
victory
ivory
forestry
perjury

treasury
memory
vapory
history
ancestry
mercury
century
armory
factory
savory
Christmas
  tree
injury
potpourri
luxury

see (sē)

1

see
(sea)

2

foresee

3

fricasee
addressee
licensee
primacy
lunacy
Holy See
courtesy
vacancy
truancy
pungency
leprosy
undersea
bankruptcy
legacy
pharmacy
papacy
fantasy
secrecy
infancy
pregnancy

buoyancy
cogency
embassy
oversee
jealousy
autopsy
Tennessee
fallacy
Christmasy
piracy
prophecy
pleurisy
stagnancy
blatancy
tangency
fluency
Argosy
privacy
regency
ecstasy

tee (tē)

1
tee
(tea)

2
settee
high tea
bootee
goatee
trustee
draftee
QT

3
absentee
appointee
deportee
fidgety
crotchety
velvety
amity
trinity
density
entity

gravity
casualty
warranty
(warrantee)
liberty
poverty
majesty
devotee
amputee
trumpety
laity
sanity
purity
sparsity
chastity
levity
cruelty
guaranty
(guarantee)
certainty
puberty
dynasty
amnesty
deputy
repartee
nicety
snippety
deity
dignity
scarcity
sanctity
cavity
brevity
faculty
sovereignty
property
sacristy
enmity
specialty

the (thē)

1
the
(thee)

3
apathy
empathy
Timothy
sympathy

vee (vē)

1
vee

3
vis-a-vis
Muscovy
eau-de-vie
c'est la vie
anchovy

we (wē)

1
we
(wee)
(oui)

3
mildewy
pillowy
meadowy
yellowy
willowy
point d'appui
shadowy
billowy
furrowy

zee (zē)

3
bourgeoisie
chimpanzee

eech (ēch)

1
each
bleach

speech
screech
beach
(beech)
reach
preach
leach
(leech)
peach
breach
(breech)
teach

2
impeach
outreach
beseech

eed (ēd)

1
bead
feed
lead
plead
Mede
(mead)
peed
greed
seed
(cede)
weed
(we'd)
heed
(he'd)
bleed
need
(knead)
(kneed)
speed
breed
creed
Swede
deed
keyed

read
(reed)
freed
treed
steed
tweed

2

Candide
nosebleed
stampede
reread
inbreed
decreed
linseed
precede
seaweed
indeed
Lockheed
mislead
impede
misread
crossbreed
hayseed
flaxseed
succeed
chickweed
pokeweed
misdeed
knock-kneed
Godspeed
agreed
reseed
(recede)
concede
milkweed
secede

3

overfeed
interbreed
pedigreed
intercede
millepede
refereed

filigreed
guaranteed
centipede
disagreed
cottonseed
supersede
tumbleweed

eef (ēf)

1

beef
reef
chief
brief
thief
leaf
grief
fief

2

relief
flyleaf
motif
belief
broadleaf

3

disbelief
misbelief
overleaf
Teneriffe
bas-relief

eek (ēk)

1

eke
beak
geek
bleak
sleek
peak
(peek)
(pique)
creek
(creak)

reek
(wreak)
sheik
(chic)
tweak
cheek
meek
freak
seek
teak
squeak
Deke
leak
(leek)
clique
sneak
speak
Greek
streak
weak
(week)
Zeke
shriek

2

technique
batik
physique
comique
unique
critique
oblique
antique

3

Mozambique
Martinique
Holy Week

eeked (ēkt)

1

eked
sneaked
reeked
(wreaked)
cheeked

peaked
(peeked)
(piqued)
shrieked
tweaked
leaked
streaked
squeaked

2

pink-cheeked
antiqued
red-cheeked

3

eagle-beaked
apple-
 cheeked
rosy-cheeked

eel (ēl)

1

eel
feel
kneel
reel
(real)
steel
(steal)
wheel
(we'll)
heel
(heal)
meal
peel
(peal)
seal
veal
deal
keel
spiel
squeal
zeal

2

mobile
congeal

oatmeal
appeal
conceal
genteel
ideal
cornmeal
anneal
repeal
unseal
Bastille
ordeal
Camille
piecemeal
chenille
singspiel
Castile
flywheel
reveal

3───────
immobile
glockenspiel
unideal
goldenseal
paddle wheel

eeled (ēld)

1───────
kneeled
shield
wield
(wheeled)
field
peeled
(pealed)
steeled
yield
keeled
sealed
squealed

2───────
afield
airfield
Mansfield
appealed

infield
outfield
repealed
revealed
cornfield
congealed
windshield
minefield

3───────
battlefield
unrepealed
Copperfield
chesterfield
unrevealed

eem (ēm)

1───────
scheme
dream
stream
steam
beam
gleam
cream
seam
(seem)
deem
ream
scream
teem
(team)
theme

2───────
moonbeam
crossbeam
regime
extreme
millstream
hornbeam
redeem
agleam
daydream
downstream
esteem

sunbeam
blaspheme
supreme
ice cream
upstream

eemed (ēmd)

1───────
beamed
gleamed
creamed
seamed
(seemed)
deemed
reamed
screamed
teemed
(teamed)
schemed
dreamed
streamed
steamed

2───────
redeemed
blasphemed
esteemed
daydreamed

een (ēn)

1───────
dean
keen
(Keene)
clean
peen
preen
sheen
queen
bean
gene
(Jean)
lean
(lien)

spleen
green
teen
wean
(ween)
glean
mean
(mien)
screen
seen
(scene)

2───────
sardine
morphine
colleen
unclean
demean
careen
terrine
sea-green
obscene
foreseen
sateen
nineteen
fourteen
routine
May Queen
phosphene
Eugene
Pauline
Kathleen
marine
Irene
tureen
gangrene
machine
fifteen
umpteen
sixteen
ravine
between
benzine
caffeine
beguine

baleen
Hellene
serene
pea-green
Racine
unseen
eighteen
canteen
thirteen
convene
cuisine
ball-peen

3 ―――――――
Aberdeen
gasoline
nectarine
figurine
evergreen
overseen
quarantine
serpentine
Florentine
intervene
gabardine
opaline
mezzanine
submarine
Nazarene
wolverine
peregrine
unforeseen
Byzantine
seventeen
Celestine
intervene
go-between
magazine
Josephine
Philippine
tangerine
tambourine
wintergreen
kerosene
velveteen

Constantine
Argentine
guillotine
Halloween
limousine
in-between

eened (ēnd)

1 ―――――――
keened
cleaned
beaned
leaned
screened
queened
fiend
gleaned
weaned

2 ―――――――
archfiend
demeaned
careened
machined
convened

eep (ēp)

1 ―――――――
cheep
(cheap)
heap
leap
peep
seep
steep
jeep
sleep
reap
weep
deep
keep
creep
sheep
sweep

2 ―――――――
upkeep
asleep
upsweep
bopeep

3 ―――――――
oversleep
chimney
  sweep

eeped (ēpt)

1 ―――――――
cheeped
leaped
seeped
heaped
peeped
steeped
reaped

eer (îr)

1 ―――――――
ear
deer
(dear)
gear
clear
smear
peer
(pier)
seer
(sear)
(sere)
steer
queer
beer
fear
here
(hear)
leer
near
spear
sheer
(shear)

weir
(we're)
cheer
sphere
jeer
blear
mere
sneer
rear
tear
(tier)
veer
year

2 ―――――――
adhere
King Lear
sincere
austere
severe
reindeer
headgear
unclear
veneer
career
cashier
revere
midyear
endear
footgear
cohere
premier
appear
uprear
frontier
brassiere

3 ―――――――
ginger beer
bombardier
hemisphere
lavalier
buccaneer
domineer
reappear
financier

gazetter
brigadier
commandeer
atmosphere
chandelier
souvenir
mountaineer
pioneer
disappear
insincere
musketeer
volunteer
yesteryear
grenadier
interfere
cavalier
gondolier
engineer
auctioneer
privateer
profiteer
persevere
stratosphere

eered (îrd)

1 ———————
feared
leered
neared
reared
tiered
(teared)
weird
beard
cleared
sneered
seared
steered
cheered
geared
smeared
peered
sheared

(sheered)
veered
queered

2 ———————
adhered
appeared
cashiered
lop-eared
Bluebeard
veneered
careered
brassiered
endeared
revered
upreared

3 ———————
commandeered
domineered
reappeared
profiteered
interfered
mountaineered
disappeared
volunteered
engineered
pioneered
privateered
persevered

eece (ēs)

1 ———————
geese
grease
(Greece)
lease
niece
(Nice)
cease
fleece
peace
(piece)
crease

2 ———————
obese
valise
Bernice
neckpiece
mouthpiece
increase
caprice
sublease
Felice
apiece
timepiece
Clarice
decease
release
police
decrease
Maurice
hair piece

3 ———————
centerpiece
frontispiece
mantelpiece
masterpiece
predecease

eest (ēst)

1 ———————
east
least
(leased)
greased
ceased
beast
fleeced
creased
feast
pieced
priest
yeast

2 ———————
northeast
released
increased

southeast
policed
archpriest
artiste
subleased
decreased
deceased

eet (ēt)

1 ———————
eat
feat
(feet)
skeet
cleat
meat
(meet)
treat
sheet
suite
(sweet)
beat
(beet)
bleat
pleat
neat
greet
street
tweet
cheat
heat
fleet
sleet
peat
(Pete)
Crete
seat
wheat

2 ———————
deadbeat
upbeat
defeat
elite
complete

sweetmeat
secrete
excrete
entreat
conceit
tout de suite
offbeat
heartbeat
reheat
delete
athlete
repeat
concrete
retreat
mistreat
reseat
unseat
drumbeat
browbeat
mesquite
deplete
mincemeat
compete
discrete
receipt
unsweet
buckwheat

3 ————
overeat
indiscrete
balance sheet
parakeet
Marguerite
county seat
incomplete
bittersweet
aquavit
easy street

eeth (ēth)

1 ————
heath
wreath

Keith
sheath
neath
teeth

2 ————
beneath
eyeteeth
bequeath

3 ————
underneath
Christmas
  wreath

eev (ēv)

1 ————
eve
heave
sleeve
grieve
leave
peeve
weave
(we've)
cleave
Steve

2 ————
naive
believe
aggrieve
deceive
perceive
achieve
relieve
reprieve
receive
qui vive
upheave
bereave
retrieve
conceive
reweave

3 ————
make-believe
interleave
reconceive
preconceive
disbelieve
misconceive
interweave

eeved (ēvd)

1 ————
heaved
peeved
cleaved
grieved
sleeved
thieved

2 ————
achieved
relieved
reprieved
received
upheaved
bereaved
retrieved
conceived
believed
aggrieved
deceived
perceived

3 ————
reconceived
misconceived
preconceived
disbelieved
interleaved
unconceived
reperceived
unperceived

eeze (ēz)

1 ————
ease
please

breeze
seize
(sees)
squeeze
cheese
sneeze
freeze
(frieze)
tease
(tees)
(teas)
wheeze
these
tweeze

2 ————
unease
chemise
appease
unfreeze
disease
displease
Burmese
trapeze
deep-freeze
Chinese
Maltese
Louise

3 ————
journalese
Androcles
Siamese
Japanese
Pekinese
Portuguese
Pericles
Cantonese
overseas
Damocles
Hercules
manganese
Viennese
antifreeze

Double ee (ē) sounds

When stars are tired of gleaming,
When I am tired of dreaming.

—*"Then I'll Be Tired Of You," lyric by E. Y. Harburg*
music by Arthur Schwartz

eeah (ē'ə)

2
Thea
Rhea
via
Leah

3
Medea
Judea
Lucia
idea
Bahia
Maria
Chaldea
Korea

eecher (ēch'ər)

2
leacher
(leecher)
reacher
screecher
bleacher
breacher
preacher
feature
creature
teacher

eeching (ēch'ĭng)

2
beaching
breaching
leaching
(leeching)
screeching
teaching
bleaching
reaching
preaching
I Ching

3
impeaching
outreaching
beseeching
far-reaching

eeded (ēd'əd)

2
beaded
pleaded
weeded
deeded
needed
(kneaded)
heeded
seeded
tweeded

3
unheeded
receded
exceeded
proceeded
stampeded
preceded
succeeded
impeded
acceded
conceded
unweeded

eeder (ēd'ər)

2
leader
cedar
(seeder)
feeder
bleeder
speeder
heeder
pleader
reader
weeder
kneader

3
bandleader
stampeder
ringleader
misleader
succeeder

eedy (ēd'ē)

2
beady
needy
greedy
weedy
speedy
tweedy
reedy
seedy

eeding (ēd'ĭng)

2
beading
leading
breeding
needing
(kneading)
feeding
bleeding
speeding
seeding
(ceding)
heeding
pleading
reading
weeding

57

3

misleading
rereading
crossbreeding
succeeding
stampeding
misreading
receding
(reseeding)
conceding
impeding
inbreeding
preceding
proceeding

**eedless
(ēd'lĭs)**

2

heedless
speedless
greedless
steedless
creedless
weedless
needless
seedless

**eeing
(ē'ĭng)**

2

being
fleeing
treeing
freeing
seeing
skiing
teeing

3

well-being
agreeing
foreseeing
decreeing

unseeing
sightseeing

**eeker
(ēk'ər)**

2

beaker
sleeker
peeker
squeaker
bleaker
meeker
speaker
shrieker
sneaker
weaker
tweaker
wreaker

**eeking
(ēk'ĭng)**

2

beaking
peaking
(peeking)
(piquing)
streaking
sleeking
speaking
creaking
seeking
tweaking
leaking
sneaking
reeking
(wreaking)
shrieking
squeaking
eking

3

self-seeking
bespeaking

**eekly
(ēk'lē)**

2

bleakly
weakly
(weekly)
sleekly
meekly

3

obliquely
uniquely
triweekly
biweekly

**eelded
(ēl'dəd)**

2

fielded
shielded
yielded
wielded

**eelding
(ēl'dĭng)**

2

fielding
yielding
shielding
wielding

eeler (ēl'ər)

2

healer
(heeler)
reeler
wheeler
dealer
peeler
sealer
feeler

stealer
squealer

eely (ēl'ē)

2

squealy
mealy
freely

**eeling
(ēl'ĭng)**

2

dealing
kneeling
sealing
(ceiling)
feeling
peeling
(pealing)
steeling
(stealing)
squealing
healing
(heeling)
reeling
wheeling

3

Darjeeling
concealing
unfeeling
appealing
congealing
repealing
revealing
annealing

**eeman
(ēm'ăn)**

2

he-man
free man
G-man
T-man

eemer
(ēm′ər)

2
beamer
schemer
creamer
reamer
screamer
steamer
femur
dreamer
seemer
(seamer)

3
redeemer
blasphemer
daydreamer
extremer

eemy
(ēm′ē)

2
beamy
Mimi
creamy
seamy
gleamy
screamy
dreamy
streamy
steamy

eeming
(ēm′ĭng)

2
beaming
gleaming
creaming
seeming
(seaming)
deeming
reaming
screaming

teeming
(teaming)
scheming
dreaming
streaming
steaming

3
redeeming
blaspheming
esteeming
daydreaming

eemless
(ēm′lĭs)

2
seamless
schemeless
creamless
themeless
dreamless
steamless

eena (ēn′ə)

2
Lena
Tina
Gina
Nina

3
galena
subpoena
marina
Christina
Athena
hyena
arena
Messina
Georgina
Paulina
farina
czarina
cantina
novena

eener
(ēn′ər)

2
keener
cleaner
screener
leaner
meaner
weaner
(wiener)
gleaner
greener

3
demeanor
serener
obscener

eenest
(ēn′ĭst)

2
keenest
meanest
leanest
cleanest
greenest

eening
(ēn′ĭng)

2
cleaning
screening
keening
meaning
weaning
leaning
greening

3
careening
subvening
demeaning
machining
well-meaning
convening

eeno (ēn′ō)

2
keno
Nino
Reno

3
casino
neutrino

eeper
(ēp′ər)

2
deeper
keeper
peeper
steeper
cheaper
leaper
reaper
weeper
sleeper
creeper
sweeper

3
bookkeeper
shopkeeper
horsekeeper
innkeeper
barkeeper
housekeeper
timekeeper
doorkeeper
gatekeeper

eepee
(ēp′ē)

2
weepy
sleepy
creepy
tepee

eeping (ēp′ĭng)

2
heaping
leaping
peeping
seeping
sleeping
reaping
weeping
keeping
creeping
sweeping
steeping

3
safekeeping
shopkeeping
housekeeping
bookkeeping
timekeeping

eeple (ēp′əl)

2
people
steeple

eerence (îr′əns)

3
adherence
coherence
appearance

eerest (îr′ist)

2
dearest
sheerest
merest
queerest
nearest
clearest

3
sincerest
austerest
severest

eerful (îr′fəl)

2
earful
cheerful
fearful
tearful

eery (îr′ē)

2
eerie
(aerie)
(Erie)
cheery
dreary
dearie
leery
weary
bleary
query

earring (îr′ĭng)

2
earring
hearing
clearing
peering
searing
steering
cheering
jeering
nearing
spearing
shearing
veering
fearing
leering
sneering
rearing
queering
tearing

3
endearing
besmearing
adhering
veneering
cashiering
cohering
appearing

earless (îr′lĭs)

2
earless
tearless
fearless
peerless
cheerless
gearless
spearless

eerly (îr′lē)

2
dearly
nearly
yearly
clearly
drearly
merely
queerly

3
sincerely
austerely
severely

eero (îr′ō)

2
hero
Nero
zero

eecer (ēs′ər)

2
leaser
creaser
fleecer
greaser

eeces (ēs′iz)

2
leases
pieces
creases
fleeces
ceases
nieces
greases

3
subleases
decreases
releases
increases
valises
caprices

eeceless (ēs′lĭs)

2
greaseless
ceaseless
creaseless
peaceless

eeted (ēt′əd)

2
cheated
sleeted
seated
heated
cleated
greeted
pleated

meted
treated
sheeted

3
defeated
unheated

repleated
competed
entreated
reheated
deleted
completed

excreted
mistreated
conceited
preheated
depleted
repeated

secreted
retreated
reseated
unseated

Triple ee (ē) sounds

In a mountain greenery,
Where God paints the scenery.

—*"Mountain Greenery," lyric by Lorenz Hart, music by*
Richard Rodgers

eechable
(ēch'əbəl)

3 —————
reachable
teachable
preachable

eedable
(ēd'əbəl)

3 —————
deedable
leadable
readable
feedable
pleadable
seedable
kneadable

eediest
(ēd'ēĭst)

3 —————
beadiest
greediest

neediest
seediest
speediest
weediest

eelable
(ēl'əbəl)

3 —————
dealable
sealable
feelable
stealable
peelable

eemable
(ēm'əbəl)

3 —————
beamable
creamable
reamable
dreamable
steamable

eeminess
(ēm'ēnĭs)

3 —————
creaminess
dreaminess
steaminess
seaminess

eerfully
(îr'fəlē)

3 —————
cheerfully
fearfully
tearfully

eezable
(ēz'əbəl)

3 —————
feasible
freezable

squeezable
seizable

eezily
(ēz'əlē)

3 —————
easily
breezily
cheesily
sleazily
queasily
weaselly

eezingly
(ēz'ĭnglē)

3 —————
pleasingly
freezingly
teasingly
wheezingly

Single eh (ĕ) sounds

Your eyes reveal that you have the soul
Of the nicest man I've met.
But how long must I play the role
of a tearful Juliet?

—"Please," lyric by Leo Robin, music by Ralph Rainger

etch (ĕch)

1
etch
fetch
ketch
sketch
retch
(wretch)
stretch
vetch
kvetch

etched (ĕcht)

1
etched
fetched
sketched
stretched
kvetched
retched

ed (ĕd)

1
Ed
bed
dead
fed
head
led
(lead)
said
spread
zed
Ted
tread
red
(read)
Ned
wed
sped
sled
stead

2
coed
hotbed
hothead
well-fed
unfed
ahead
deadhead
redhead
behead
blockhead
bullhead
drumhead
bonehead
drop dead
spearhead
forehead
sorehead
bobsled
mislead
pre-med
highbred
homebred
inbred
purebred
crossbred
sweetbread
shortbread
truebred
widespread
outspread
retread
bloodshed
homestead
instead
rewed
unwed

3
underfed
Marblehead
fountainhead
arrowhead
loggerhead
copperhead
overhead
figurehead
thoroughbred
gingerbread
underspread
overspread
watershed

ef (ĕf)

1
deaf
clef
ref.
chef

egg (ĕg)

1
beg
keg
leg
egg
peg
yegg

edge (ĕj)

1
edge
hedge
ledge
fledge
pledge
wedge
dredge
sedge

2
allege

63

edged (ĕjd)

1

edged
hedged
ledged
pledged
dredged
wedged
fledged

2

alleged
unpledged

eck (ĕk)

1

check
deck
heck
neck
peck
speck
(spec)
wreck
trek
tech
beck
fleck

2

home-ec
roughneck
henpeck
shipwreck
high tech

3

countercheck
bottleneck
rubberneck
leatherneck

ex (ĕks)

1

specks
(specs)

wrecks
sex
vex
flex
(flecks)
Tex
treks
checks
decks
necks
pecks
hex

2

index
reflex
complex
perplex
duplex
annex
apex
vortex
convex

ext (ĕkst)

1

next
sexed
text
vexed
hexed

2

annexed
perplexed
pretext
context
indexed

ecked (ĕkt)

1

checked
decked
necked
pecked

wrecked
sect
trekked
flecked
specked

2

unchecked
affect
effect
defect
prefect
infect
perfect
subject
eject
reject
inject
project
elect
select
reflect
neglect
collect
connect
respect
inspect
insect
prospect
expect
suspect
erect
direct
correct
disect
detect
protect

3

disinfect
interject
dialect
re-elect
intelect
genuflect
recollect

disconnect
self-respect
disrespect
retrospect
introspect
indirect
misdirect
incorrect
resurrect
intersect
architect

ects (ĕkts)

2

affects
effects
defects
infects
perfects
subjects
ejects
rejects
injects
disects
elects
selects
reflects
neglects
collects
respects
connects
inspects
prospects
expects
suspects
corrects
disects
detects
protects

3

interjects
dialects
re-elects
intellects

genuflects
recollects
reconnects
disconnects
disrespects
retrospects
introspects
misdirects
architects
intersects

el (ĕl)

1

el
bell
(belle)
dell
fell
hell
gel
smell
spell
sell
(cell)
shell
tell
well
dwell
swell
yell

2

rebel
bluebell
cowbell
pell-mell
noel
lapel
repel
compel
propel
expel
misspell
resell
excel

hotel
cartel
foretell
farewell
dispel

3

Annabel
Isabell
Jezebel
citadel
infidel
parallel
nonpareil
undersell
oversell
carousel
cockelshell

eld (ĕld)

1

held
meld
smelled
shelled
spelled
swelled
weld
dwelled
quelled
yelled

2

rebelled
beheld
upheld
withheld
repelled
compelled
propelled
misspelled
expelled
dispelled
excelled

elf (ĕlf)

1

elf
self
shelf

2

myself
thyself
himself
oneself
herself
yourself
itself

elm (ĕlm)

1

elm
helm
realm
whelm

3

overwhelm

elp (ĕlp)

1

help
yelp
kelp

elt (ĕlt)

1

belt
dealt
felt
melt
smelt
pelt
svelte
welt
dwelt

elth (ĕlth)

1

health
stealth
wealth

elv (ĕlv)

1

delve
shelve
twelve

elves (ĕlvz)

1

elves
selves
shelves
delves

2

themselves
ourselves
yourselves

em (ĕm)

1

hem
gem
crème
stem
them

empt (ĕmpt)

2

attempt
exempt
pre-empt

en (ĕn)

1

den
ten
hen

pen
wren
then
when
yen
Zen
Ken
men

2 ────────
Big Ben
again
amen
horsemen
bushmen
Norsemen
pigpen

3 ────────
oxygen
nitrogen
specimen
gentlemen
aldermen
Englishmen
julienne
fountain pen
poison-pen
denizen
citizen

ench (ĕnch)

1 ────────
clench
drench
French
trench
wrench
stench
wench
quench

2 ────────
entrench
workbench

end (ĕnd)

1 ────────
end
bend
lend
blend
mend
penned
spend
friend
trend
send
tend
wend

2 ────────
unbend
defend
amend
commend
append
depend
expend
suspend
befriend
ascend
descend
Godsend
transcend
attend
pretend
intend
contend
extend

3 ────────
dividend
apprehend
comprehend
recommend
reverend
condescend

ength (ĕngkth)

1 ────────
length
strength

ence (ĕns)

1 ────────
dense
fence
hence
pence
sense
tense
whence

2 ────────
condense
defense
offense
immense
commence
sixpence
dispense
expense
suspense
incense
nonsense
pretense
intense

3 ────────
confidence
residence
evidence
providence
impudence
self-defence
negligence
diligence
audience
excellence
prevalence
pestilence

violence
insolence
turbulence
succulence
fraudulence
opulence
permanence
eminence
imminence
prominence
pertinence
abstinence
difference
reference
preference
conference
reverence
innocence
frankincense
common
  sense
confidence
impotence
affluence
influence
subsequence
consequence
eloquence
dissidence
dissonance
recompense

enced (ĕnst)

2 ────────
against
condensed
commenced
dispensed
incensed

3 ────────
recompensed
influenced

ent (ĕnt)

1

bent
dent
gent
Kent
lent
meant
spent
rent
sent
(scent)
(cent)
tent
vent
went

2

unbent
indent
relent
lament
cement
augment
ferment
torment
repent
unspent
resent
present
ascent
decent
unsent
intent
content
extent
event
prevent
frequent
invent
advent

3

accident
incident
confident
evident
provident
negligent
diligent
excellent
insolent
turbulent
succulent
fraudulent
opulent
imminent
parliament
ornament
tournament
sacrament
testament
management
implement
supplement
tenement
excrement
banishment
punishment
nourishment
ravishment
sediment
condiment
rudiment
regiment
compliment
(complement)
government
document
argument
instrument
monument
permanent
emminent
circumvent
underwent

represent
subsequent

ep (ĕp)

1

prep
pep
step
yep

2

instep
stair step
misstep
footstep

ept (ĕpt)

1

kept
slept
crept
wept
swept
leapt

2

adept
inept
accept
precept
concept
unswept
upswept

ess (ĕs)

1

Bess
chess
fess
guess
less
bless
mess

dress
press
stress
Tess
yes

2

confess
profess
unless
finesse
caress
address
headdress
redress
undress
egress
regress
progress
transgress
depress
repress
impress
compress
oppress
express
suppress
distress
assess
obsess
success
recess
princess
possess
digress

3

SOS
stewardess
shepherdess
convalesce
nonetheless
baroness
phosphoresce
overstress

reassess
repossess
dispossess
poetess
effervesce

esk (ĕsk)

1

desk

2

burlesque
grotesque

3

gigantesque
picturesque
arabesque
statuesque

est (ĕst)

1

best
chest
guest
(guessed)
jest
(geste)
blessed
nest
pest
rest
breast
dressed
crest
stressed
test
vest
west
quest
zest
messed
fessed

2

suggest
digest
ingest
beau geste
Celeste
molest
arrest
caressed
headrest
unrest
footrest
abreast
addressed
undressed
digressed
transgressed
progressed
depressed
repressed
compressed
oppressed
suppressed
expressed
distressed
recessed
possessed
attest
detest
contest
divest
invest
bequest
request
inquest
Midwest
Northwest
Southwest
behest

3

manifest
Budapest

Bucharest
readdressed
interest
effervesced
reassessed
repossessed
self-possessed
unpossessed
depossessed

et (ĕt)

1

bet
debt
get
jet
let
net
fret
threat
set
stet
vet
wet
sweat
yet

2

cadet
Tibet
indebt
Claudette
Odette
beget
forget
croquette
coquette
sublet
toilette
roulette
Nanette
brunet

regret
beset
inset
sunset
subset
outset
brochette
duet
vignette

3

Juliet
etiquette
novelette
clarinet
bassinet
Antoinette
minuet
cigarette
leatherette
silhouette
pirouette
statuette
heavyset

eth (ĕth)

1

death
breath
Seth
Beth

3

twentieth
thirtieth
fortieth
fiftieth
sixtieth
eightieth
ninetieth

Double eh (ĕ) sounds

Don't start collecting things.
Give me my rose and my glove.
Sweetheart, they're suspecting things,
People will say we're in love.

—"People Will Say We're in Love," lyric by Oscar
  Hammerstein II, music by Richard Rodgers

**ebble
(ĕb′əl)**

2 ——————
pebble
rebel
treble

**etcher
(ĕch′ər)**

2 ——————
sketcher
lecher
Fletcher
stretcher

**etching
(ĕch′ĭng)**

2 ——————
etching
fetching
sketching
stretching
retching
kvetching

**edded
(ĕd′ĭd)**

2 ——————
headed
leaded
sledded
breaded
shredded
threaded
dreaded
bedded
treaded
wedded

3 ——————
imbedded
hardheaded
beheaded
pigheaded
thickheaded
coolheaded
bullheaded
bareheaded
flatheaded
lightheaded
softheaded
hotheaded
unwedded

**edder
(ĕd′ər)**

2 ——————
Cheddar
deader
header
redder
spreader
shredder
threader

eddy (ĕd′ē)

2 ——————
eddy
ready
Freddy
Teddy
steady

3 ——————
already
unready
unsteady

**edding
(ĕd′ĭng)**

2 ——————
bedding
heading
sledding
dreading
breading
spreading
shredding
threading
treading
shedding
wedding

3 ——————
homesteading
beheading

**eddly
(ĕd′lē)**

2 ——————
deadly
medley

**eddline
(ĕd′līn)**

2 ——————
deadline
headline
breadline

**eddlock
(ĕd′lŏk)**

2 ——————
deadlock
headlock
wedlock

**egging
(ĕg′ĭng)**

2 ——————
egging
begging
legging
pegging

edges
(ĕj′ĭz)

2

edges
hedges
ledges
fledges
pledges
dredges
wedges

edging
(ĕj′ĭng)

2

edging
hedging
fledging
pledging
wedging

3

alleging

eckless
(ĕk′lĭs)

2

feckless
necklace
(neckless)
reckless

ekshun
(ĕk′shən)

2

section

3

affection
reflection
deflection
infection
confection
perfection
ejection
rejection

injection
projection
erection
selection
inflection
complexion
connection
inspection
direction
correction
detection
protection
election
defection
dejection
dissection

ected
(ĕk′tĭd)

3

affected
effected
infected
perfected
defected
objected
subjected
ejected
dejected
rejected
injected
projected
elected
selected
deflected
reflected
inflected
neglected
collected
connected
respected
erected
detected
directed

protected
corrected
dissected
expected
inspected
suspected

ecter
(ĕk′tər)

2

nectar
sector
vector
hector

3

objector
injector
elector
selector
deflector
reflector
collector
connector
inspector
erector
director
corrector
protector

ecting
(ĕk′tĭng)

3

affecting
defecting
effecting
infecting
perfecting
objecting
subjecting
ejecting
rejecting
injecting
projecting
electing

selecting
deflecting
reflecting
neglecting
collecting
connecting
inspecting
expecting
suspecting
erecting
directing
correcting
dissecting
detecting
protecting

ective
(ĕk′tĭv)

3

effective
affective
defective
invective
objective
subjective
elective
selective
reflective
collective
connective
respective
prospective
perspective
directive
corrective
detective
protective

ella (ĕl′ə)

2

Ella
Bella
fella

3

rubella
umbrella

eller (ĕl′ər)

2

feller
teller
speller
seller
(cellar)
stellar
dweller
yeller

3

dispeller
exceller
foreteller
cave dweller
propeller

elly (ĕl′ē)

2

Elly
belly
Delhi
jelly
Kelly
smelly
Nelly
Shelly
telly

3

potbelly

elling
(ĕl′ĭng)

2

spelling
selling
shelling
telling

dwelling
swelling
quelling
yelling
jelling
knelling
felling

3

rebelling
repelling
compelling
propelling
dispelling
misspelling
expelling
excelling
foretelling

ello (ĕl′ō)

2

bellow
cello
fellow
Jell-O
mellow
yellow
hello

elted
(ĕl′tĭd)

2

belted
melted
smelted
pelted

elter (ĕl′tər)

2

smelter
shelter
swelter

elting
(ĕl′tĭng)

2

belting
melting
smelting
pelting

ember
(ĕm′bər)

2

ember
member

3

remember
December
September
November
dismember

empted
(ĕmp′təd)

3

pre-empted
exempted
attempted

empting
(ĕmp′tĭng)

3

pre-empting
exempting
attempting

ended
(ĕn′dĭd)

2

ended
blended
mended
tended
vended
wended

3

defended
offended
unblended
amended
depended
befriended
ascended
descended
transcended
attended
pretended
intended
contended
extended

endent
(ĕn′dənt)

2

descendant
ascendant
dependent

ender
(ĕn′dər)

2

bender
fender
gender
lender
blender
splendor
slender
mender
render
sender
tender
vender

3

defender
offender
surrender
pretender
contender

**ending
(ĕn′dĭng)**

2

ending
bending
lending
blending
mending
pending
spending
sending
vending
tending
wending
fending

3

unbending
defending
amending
commending
depending
suspending
befriending
ascending
descending
transcending
attending
pretending
contending
extending

**endless
(ĕnd′lĭs)**

2

endless
friendless

enny (ĕn′ē)

2

any
Benny
Jenny
Lenny

many
penny

3

halfpenny
sixpenny

**ennis
(ĕn′ĭs)**

2

Dennis
menace
tennis
Venice

**enser
(ĕn′sər)**

2

denser
Spencer
censor
(censer)
(sensor)
tenser

3

condenser
dispenser
intenser

**enshul
(ĕn′shəl)**

3

credential
torrential
essential
potential
sequential

**enshun
(ĕn′shən)**

2

mention
tension

3

dimension
suspension
ascension
detention
attention
retention
intention
pretension
extension
prevention
invention
convention

**encil
(ĕn′səl)**

2

pencil
stencil
tensile

3

prehensile

**ensing
(ĕn′sĭng)**

3

commencing
condensing
dispensing
incensing

**ensive
(ĕn′sĭv)**

3

expensive
defensive
offensive
intensive
extensive

entle (ĕnt′l)

2

dental
gentle
mental

3

fragmental
segmental
percentile

**ented
(ĕn′təd)**

2

dented
rented
scented
vented

3

indented
relented
lamented
demented
cemented
augmented
fermented
tormented
repented
unrented
consented
unscented
contented
prevented
invented

**enter
(ĕn′tər)**

2

enter
center
renter

3

re-enter
lamenter
cementer
tormentor
repenter
frequenter
inventor
presenter

**enting
(ĕn′tĭng)**

2

denting
renting
scenting
venting

3

indenting
relenting
lamenting
cementing
augmenting
fomenting
fermenting
tormenting
repenting
assenting
preventing
inventing
frequenting
presenting

**entless
(ĕnt′lĭs)**

2

scentless

3

relentless
eventless

**epshun
(ĕp′shən)**

3

conception
reception
exception
deception
perception

erry (ĕr′ē)

2

berry
(bury)
ferry
merry
Sherry
(cheri)
very
Perry
Terry
cherry

3

bayberry
blueberry
blackberry
cranberry
strawberry
raspberry
gooseberry

**errick
(ĕr′ĭk)**

2

Eric
derrick
cleric

3

Homeric
generic
hysteric

**erreez
(ĕr′ēz)**

2

berries
(buries)
cherries
ferries

3

bayberries
blueberries
blackberries
cranberries
strawberries
raspberries
gooseberries

**esjun
(ĕs′chən)**

3

suggestion
digestion
ingestion
congestion

**essence
(ĕs′əns)**

2

essence

3

quiescence
fluorescence
excrescence

**essent
(ĕs′ənt)**

2 crescent

3

fluorescent
quiescent
incessant
excrescent
depressant

esser (ĕs′ər)

2

dresser
lesser

3

confessor
professor
compressor
oppressor
suppresser
successor
possessor

**esses
(ĕs′ĭz)**

2

guesses
blesses
messes
dresses
presses
stresses
yeses
fesses

3

confesses
professes
finesses
caresses
addresses
undresses

regresses
digresses
transgresses
progresses
represses
impresses
compresses
oppresses
suppresses
expresses
distresses
successes

eshun
(ĕsh′ən)

2
Hessian
freshen
session

3
confession
oppression
profession
progression
digression
aggression
transgression
depression
impression
regression
expression
obsession
recession
succession
possession

essing
(ĕs′ĭng)

2
guessing
blessing
messing
pressing

stressing
yessing
fessing

3
confessing
professing
caressing
addressing
undressing
digressing
progressing
depressing
repressing
impressing
compressing
oppressing
suppressing
expressing
possessing
distressing

essive
(ĕs′ĭv)

3
aggressive
progressive
repressive
impressive
oppressive
suppressive
recessive
excessive
successive

essel (ĕs′əl)

2
nestle
wrestle
vessel

ested
(ĕs′tĭd)

2
jested
nested
rested
tested
vested
bested
crested

3
infested
suggested
digested
ingested
congested
molested
arrested
unrested
attested
detested
protested
requested
divested
invested

ester
(ĕs′tər)

2
Esther
Chester
Hester
jester
Lester
nester
pester
rester
tester
quester

3
molester
trimester
contester

protester
sequester
Sylvester
Northwester
Southwester
investor

esting
(ĕs′tĭng)

2
jesting
nesting
resting
cresting
testing
vesting
questing

3
investing
suggesting
digesting
congesting
arresting
attesting
detesting
contesting
protesting
divesting
investing
requesting

etted
(ĕt′ĭd)

3
abetted
indebted
unfretted
regretted

etter (ĕt′ər)

2
better
(bettor)

74

debtor
wetter
sweater
fetter
fretter
setter

3
abettor
go-getter
dead letter
typesetter
red-letter

**ether
(ĕth′ər)**

2
feather
heather
leather
weather
(whether)

3
pinfeather
together
bellwether

**ethered
(ĕth′ərd)**

2
feathered
leathered
weathered

etty (ĕt′ē)

2
Betty
Nettie
petty
sweaty
Getty

3
confetti
spaghetti
libretti

**ettick
(ĕt′ĭk)**

3
pathetic
synthetic
aesthetic
poetic
cosmetic
genetic
magnetic
phonetic

**etting
(ĕt′ĭng)**

2
betting
getting
letting
netting

fretting
setting
sweating

3
abetting
forgetting
regretting
upsetting

ettel (ĕt′əl)

2
metal
(mettle)
petal
settle
nettle

etto (ĕt′ō)

2
ghetto

3
falsetto
larghetto

ever (ĕv′ər)

2
ever
never

3
whichever
whenever

wherever
forever
whatever
however
endeavor

evvy (ĕv′ē)

2
Chevy
heavy
levy
bevy

**ezents
(ĕz′əns)**

2
peasants
presents
(presence)

**ezhur
(ĕzh′ər)**

2
pleasure
measure
treasure
leisure

Triple eh (ĕ) sounds

We in sincerity
Wish you prosperity

—*from* The Gondoliers, *lyric by W. S. Gilbert, music*
by Arthur Sullivan

edible
(ĕd'əbəl)

3 ———————
edible
credible
spreadable
weddable
beddable

eddier
(ĕd'ēər)

3 ———————
readier
steadier

eddiest
(ĕd'ēəst)

3 ———————
readiest
steadiest

eddicate
(ĕd'əkāt)

3 ———————
dedicate
medicate
predicate

eddily
(ĕd'əlē)

3 ———————
readily
steadily

editor
(ĕd'ətər)

3 ———————
editor
creditor

efference
(ĕf'ərəns)

3 ———————
reference
preference
deference

eckoning
(ĕk'ənĭng)

3 ———————
beckoning
reckoning

ellable
(ĕl'əbəl)

3 ———————
spellable
sellable

tellable
quellable

elleton
(ĕl'ətən)

3 ———————
skeleton
gelatin

ellegate
(ĕl'əgāt)

3 ———————
delegate
relegate

ellower
(ĕl'ōər)

3 ———————
mellower
yellower
bellower

ellowest
(ĕl'ōəst)

3 ———————
mellowest
yellowest

eltering
(ĕl'tərĭng)

3 ———————
sheltering
sweltering

elthier
(ĕl'thēər)

3 ———————
healthier
wealthier
stealthier

elthiest
(ĕl'thēĭst)

3 ———————
healthiest
wealthiest
stealthiest

ellusly
(ĕl'əslē)

3 ———————
jealously
zealously

emery
(ĕm'ərē)

3 ———————
emery
memory

76

endable
(ĕn′dəbəl)

3
endable
lendable
mendable
bendable
sendable

enderest
(ĕn′dərəst)

3
slenderest
tenderest

endlessly
(ĕnd′lĭslē)

3
endlessly
friendlessly

endlessness
(ĕnd′lĭsnĭs)

3
endlessness
friendlessness

enerate
(ĕn′ərāte)

3
generate
venerate

entering
(ĕn′tərĭng)

3
entering
centering

errier
(ĕr′ēər)

3
burier
merrier
terrier

errishing
(ĕr′ĭshĭng)

3
cherishing
perishing

ethery
(ĕth′ərē)

3
feathery
heathery
leathery

ethering
(ĕth′ərĭng)

3
feathering
weathering

everence
(ĕv′ərəns)

3
reverence
severance

everest
(ĕv′ərĭst)

3
Everest
cleverest

everage
(ĕv′ərĭj)

3
beverage
leverage

evity
(ĕv′ətē)

3
levity
brevity

esentry
(ĕz′əntrē)

3
pleasantry
peasantry

esidents
(ĕz′ədĕns)

3
residents
(residence)
presidents

esident
(ĕz′ədĕnt)

3
resident
president

Single eye (ī) sounds

I need no soft lights to enchant me,
If you'll only grant me the right
To hold you ever so tight'
And to feel in the night
The nearness of you.

—"The Nearness of You," lyric by Ned Washington,
music by Hoagy Carmichael

eye (ī)

1
aye
(eye)

2
red-eye
black eye
pinkeye
buckeye
fisheye
cat's-eye

by (bī)

1
by
(bye)
(buy)

2
good-by
bye-bye
hereby
thereby
whereby

3
by and by
rockaby
lullaby
hushaby
underbuy
overbuy

alibi
passerby
passersby

die (dī)

1
die
(dye)

fie (fī)

3
stupefy
putrefy
liquefy
edify
modify
qualify
nullify
amplify
simplify
mummify
magnify
dignify
unify
clarify
verify
terrify
horrify
glorify
petrify
purify
pacify

specify
classify
falsify
rectify
crucify
gratify
sanctify
certify
fortify
mortify
testify
justify
mystify
beautify
satisfy
calcify
ratify
ossify
notify

lie (lī)

1
lie
(lye)
fly
ply
sly

2
ally
rely
gadfly
horsefly

housefly
shoofly
apply
reply
imply
comply
supply
July
firefly

3
dragonfly
butterfly
reapply
misapply
multiply
underlie
overlie

pie (pī)

1
pie
(pi)
spy

2
magpie
potpie
mince pie

3
humble pie
apple pie
occupy

rye (rī)

1

rye
(wry)
dry
fry
cry
pry
spry
try

2

fish fry
decry
outcry
descry
awry

tie (tī)

1

tie
sty

2

hog-tie
untie
necktie
pigsty

ibe (īb)

1

bribe
scribe
tribe

2

imbibe
ascribe
subscribe
describe
prescribe
transcribe
inscribe
proscribe

ibed (ībd)

2

imbibed
subscribed
inscribed
prescribed
described
ascribed
transcribed
proscribed

ide (īd)

1

I'd
(eyed)
bide
chide
died
(dyed)
guide
hide
lied
Clyde
glide
slide
snide
spied
ride
bride
cried
dried
pried
(pride)
tried
stride
side
(sighed)
tide
(tied)
wide

2

red-eyed
black-eyed

cock-eyed
hawk-eyed
blue-eyed
abide
confide
misguide
rawhide
cowhide
bromide
denied
child bride
brown-eyed
green-eyed
untried
astride
aside
wayside
subside
bedside
broadside
beside
decide
seaside
reside
preside
offside
lakeside
hillside
inside
topside
outside
Yuletide
divide
provide
worldwide
high tide
low tide

3

bona fide
stupefied
putrefied
liquefied
pacified

specified
calcified
classified
crucified
edified
modified
qualified
nullified
magnified
dignified
glorified
terrified
petrified
purified
falsified
ossified
ratified
gratified
rectified
sanctified
notified
certified
mortified
testified
justified
mystified
beautified
satisfied
eagle-eyed
goggle-eyed
evil-eyed
misapplied
multiplied
cyanide
occupied
herbicide
fungicide
homicide
countryside
suicide
oceanside
mountainside
coincide
underside
waterside

riverside
Whitsuntide
nationwide
fireside

ife (īf)

1
life
knife
strife
wife
rife

2
jackknife
housewife
fishwife
midwife

3
afterlife
bowie knife
pocketknife

ike (īk)

1
bike
dike
hike
like
Mike
pike
spike
strike
tyke
shrike

2
Vandyke
alike
hitchhike
childlike
godlike
lifelike
unlike

dislike
turnpike

ile (īl)

1
isle
(aisle)
(I'll)
bile
guile
file
mile
smile
pile
tile
style
vile
while
(wile)

2
defile
profile
beguile
senile
compile
exile
Gentile
reptile
turnstile
hostile
futile
revile
awhile
meanwhile
worthwhile

3
crocodile
juvenile
domicile
reconcile
volatile
versatile
mercantile
infantile

iled (īld)

1
child
filed
mild
smiled
styled
wild
(whiled)
piled

2
grandchild
godchild
defiled
beguiled
compiled
self-styled
reviled
exiled

3
reconciled
domiciled

ime (īm)

1
I'm
chime
dime
lime
climb
(clime)
slime
mime
rhyme
(rime)
crime
grime
prime
time
(thyme)

2
sublime
daytime

playtime
bedtime
lifetime
springtime
meantime
noontime
sometime
nighttime

3
maritime
pantomime
summertime
aftertime
overtime

imed (īmd)

1
chimed
climbed
mimed
rhymed
primed
timed

ine (īn)

1
fine
line
mine
nine
pine
stein
Rhine
brine
shrine
shine
spine
tine
vine
wine
(whine)
swine
twine

2

combine
carbine
turbine
define
refine
confine
align
malign
headline
airline
hairline
decline
incline
feline
gold mine
carmine
canine
benign
bovine
recline
quinine
alpine
lupine
enshrine
assign
design
resign
cosign
consign
moonshine
sunshine
outshine
divine
entwine

3

concubine
realign
alkaline
crystalline
underline
calamine
undermine
porcupine

countersign
Argentine
valentine
turpentine
Palestine
Philistine
Brandywine
intertwine
auld lang
   syne

ined (īnd)

1

bind
find
(fined)
hind
kind
lined
blind
mind
(mined)
grind
signed
wined
(whined)
rind
pined

2

combined
defined
refined
behind
mankind
unkind
aligned
maligned
unlined
declined
reclined
inclined
unwind
entwined
divined

designed
resigned
cosigned
consigned

3

humankind
realigned
disinclined
color blind
underlined
mastermind
undersigned
countersigned
intertwined
womankind

ipe (īp)

1

snipe
pipe
ripe
gripe
tripe
stripe
type
wipe
swipe

2

pitch pipe
windpipe
bagpipe
blowpipe
retype
sideswipe

3

overripe
Teletype
Linotype
underripe

iped (īpt)

1

typed
wiped
swiped
griped
striped
sniped
piped

2

retyped
sideswiped

ire (īr)

1

fire
hire
lyre
mire
sire
wire
choir
squire
ire
dire
tire

2

backfire
wildfire
shellfire
bonfire
misfire
spitfire
rehire
admire
aspire
expire
inspire
conspire
perspire
desire
attire
retire

barbwire
rewire
acquire
require
inquire
esquire
transpire

ired (īrd)

1

fired
hired
sired
tired
wired
squired
mired

2

backfired
misfired
admired
aspired
expired
transpired
inspired
conspired
perspired
desired
attired
retired
rewired
acquired
required
inquired
rehired

3

overtired
uninspired
undesired

ice (īs)

1

ice
dice

lice
splice
slice
mice
nice
spice
rice
price
thrice
vice
twice

2

suffice
allspice
precise
concise
entice
advice
device

3

paradise
sacrifice
edelweiss

ite (īt)

1

bite
fight
height
kite
light
blight
flight
plight
slight
mite
(might)
smite
night
(knight)
spite
rite
(right)
(write)

bright
sprite
trite
sight
(site)
(cite)
tight
quite
white

2

indict
graphite
cockfight
bullfight
fistfight
Shiite
daylight
red light
floodlight
delight
twilight
skylight
green light
moonlight
sunlight
polite
lamplight
spotlight
stoplight
starlight
flashlight
footlight
Semite
termite
midnight
good night
tonight
fortnight
unite
despite
playwright
downright
upright
cartwright

birthright
outright
eyesight
insight
(incite)
foresight
excite
airtight
requite
invite
bobwhite
hindsight
recite
ignite

3

extradite
expedite
neophyte
fahrenheit
Israelite
candlelight
satellite
impolite
dynamite
stalagmite
stalactite
overnight
day and night
reunite
copyright
underwrite
overwrite
parasite
oversight
second sight
appetite

ive (īv)

1

I've
chive
dive
five
hive

jive
live
drive
strive
thrive

2

swan dive
nose dive
beehive
alive
arrive
deprive
contrive
revive
survive

3

overdrive

ize (īz)

1

guise
rise
prize
size
wise

2

disguise
demise

despise
arise
sunrise
moonrise
comprise
uprise
surprise
excise
baptize
chastise
advise
revise
devise
likewise
clockwise
unwise
crosswise
first prize
surmise
capsize
apprise

3

subsidize
oxidize
standardize
jeopardize
eulogize
energize
sympathize
verbalize
legalize

specialize
socialize
moralize
sterilize
neutralize
centralize
tantalize
stabilize
fossilize
fertilize
utilize
civilize
symbolize
idolize
victimize
compromise
mechanize
recognize
feminize
scrutinize
agonize
colonize
harmonize
modernize
fraternize
immunize
burglarize
mesmerize
satirize
theorize
authorize
memorize

vaporize
terrorize
enterprise
pasteurize
emphasize
publicize
dramatize
magnetize
sensitize
hypnotize
otherwise
tenderize
winterize

ized (īzd)

2

disguised
demised
surmised
apprised
comprised
surprised
capsized
baptized
chastised
advised
devised
revised
excised
despised

Double eye (ī) sounds

I've lived a life that's full,
I traveled each and every highway,
And more, much more than this,
I did it my way.

—"My Way," lyric by Paul Anka, music by J. Revaux
   and C. Francoix

ial (ī'əl)

2
dial
trial
vial

3
sundial
denial
mistrial

iam (ī'ăm)

2
I am
Siam

iance (ī'əns)

3
defiance
alliance
reliance
appliance
compliance

iant (ī'ənt)

2
giant
client
Bryant

3
defiant
reliant
compliant

ibal (īb'əl)

2
bible
tribal
libel

iber (īb'ər)

2
fiber
briber
Tiber

3
imbiber
subscriber
prescriber
transcriber

ibing (īb'ĭng)

3
imbibing
subscribing
describing
prescribing
transcribing
inscribing
proscribing

iball (īb'ôl)

2
eyeball
highball
fly ball

ided (īd'ĭd)

2
chided
guided
glided
prided
sided
tided
bided

3
abided
confided
misguided
collided
decided
lopsided
one-sided
two-sided
divided
presided
derided
provided

ider (īd'ər)

2
glider
spider
rider
strider
cider
wider

3
confider
backslider
roughrider
decider
insider
outsider
provider

iding (īd'ĭng)

2
chiding
guiding
hiding
gliding
sliding
riding
striding
siding
tiding
biding

3

abiding
confiding
misguiding
colliding
backsliding
subsiding
dividing
providing
residing
presiding

ier (ī′ər)

2

buyer
higher
liar
flier
plier
(plyer)
briar
dryer
friar
(fryer)
crier
prior
(pryer)
sprier

3

supplier
denier
greenbrier
sweetbrier

iest (ī′ĭst)

2

highest
sliest
driest
shiest
spriest

iet (ī′ət)

2

diet
riot
quiet

ifen (īf′ən)

2

hyphen
siphon

ifer (īf′ər)

2

lifer
knifer
cipher

ifel (īf′əl)

2

Eiffel
rifle
trifle
stifle

ifeless (īf′lĭs)

2

lifeless
knifeless
strifeless
wifeless

ifelike (īf′līk)

2

lifelike
knifelike
wifelike

i-ide (ī′īd)

2

sly-eyed
dry-eyed
pie-eyed

i-ing (ī′ĭng)

2

eyeing
buying
dying
(dyeing)
lying
flying
plying
spying
drying
frying
crying
prying
trying
sighing
tying
vying

3

defying
allying
relying
applying
replying
implying
complying
supplying
denying
untying
decrying

iking (īk′ĭng)

2

liking
spiking

striking
viking
hiking
biking

3

hitchhiking
disliking

island (īl′ənd)

2

island
highland
Thailand

3

Rhode Island
Long Island

ilder (īl′dər)

2

milder
wilder

ildest (īl′dĭst)

2

mildest
wildest

ildish (īl′dĭsh)

2

childish
mildish
wildish

ildly (īld′lē)

2

mildly
wildly

88

**ildlike
(īld'līk)**

2 ────────
childlike

**ildness
(īld'nĭs)**

2 ────────
mildness
wildness

iler (īl'ər)

2 ────────
smiler
Tyler
viler

3 ────────
beguiler
compiler
reviler

**iling
(īl'ĭng)**

2 ────────
smiling
tiling
styling
filing
riling
wiling
(whiling)

3 ────────
beguiling
compiling
exiling
restyling
reviling
unsmiling

**imer
(īm'ər)**

2 ────────
climber
mimer
primer
timer

3 ────────
sublimer
old-timer

imy (īm'ē)

2 ────────
slimy
stymie

**iming
(īm'ĭng)**

2 ────────
climbing
chiming
rhyming
priming
timing
miming

**imeless
(īm'lĭs)**

2 ────────
chimeless
dimeless
rhymeless
timeless
grimeless
slimeless

**inded
(īn'dəd)**

2 ────────
blinded
minded

3 ────────
snow-blinded
reminded
free-minded
strong-
    minded
weak-minded
like-minded

**inder
(īn'dər)**

2 ────────
binder
finder
kinder
grinder
blinder

3 ────────
bookbinder
spellbinder
pathfinder
reminder

**inding
(īn'dĭng)**

2 ────────
binding
finding
blinding
minding
winding
grinding

3 ────────
reminding
unwinding
nonbinding

**indness
(īnd'nĭs)**

2 ────────
kindness
blindness

iner (īn'ər)

2 ────────
diner
finer
liner
miner
(minor)
Shriner
signer
shiner
whiner

3 ────────
refiner
maligner
headliner
streamliner
recliner
assigner
cosigner
diviner
designer
definer

iness (īn'ĭs)

2 ────────
highness
slyness
dryness
spryness
shyness

**ining
(īn'ĭng)**

2 ────────
dining
lining
mining
signing
shining
wining
(whining)

89

3

combining
defining
refining
confining
reclining
declining
inclining
resigning
designing
outshining
entwining
assigning
cosigning
divining
headlining
streamlining

**ineless
(īn′lĭs)**

2

spineless
wineless
vineless

inely (īn′lē)

2

finely

3

benignly
divinely
malignly

**inement
(īn′mənt)**

3

refinement
confinement
alignment
enshrinement
assignment

iper (īp′ər)

2

sniper
piper
griper
viper
wiper
swiper
hyper

3

sandpiper
bagpiper
sideswiper

**iping
(īp′ĭng)**

2

typing
swiping
wiping
griping
striping
piping
sniping

3

retyping
sideswiping

**iring
(īr′ĭng)**

2

firing
hiring
tiring
wiring
squiring

3

admiring
aspiring
expiring
conspiring
perspiring

retiring
acquiring
inquiring
desiring
backfiring
misfiring
rehiring
rewiring
transpiring
inspiring
attiring

**ireless
(īr′lĭs)**

2

tireless
wireless
fireless

irely (īr′lē)

2

direly

3

entirely

icer (īs′ər)

2

dicer
slicer
splicer
nicer
ricer

3

preciser
conciser
enticer

ices (īs′ĭz)

2

ices
dices
slices

splices
spices
prices
vices

3

suffices
entices
devices

**icing
(īs′ĭng)**

2

icing
dicing
slicing
splicing
pricing

**iceless
(īs′lĭs)**

2

iceless
spiceless
riceless
priceless
viceless

ited (īt′əd)

2

lighted
blighted
slighted
knighted
spited
sighted
(cited)
righted

3

indicted
delighted
ignited
united
recited

excited
incited
farsighted
clearsighted
nearsighted
shortsighted
requited
invited
benighted
floodlighted
spotlighted

iten (īt′n)

2
heighten
lighten
brighten
frighten
tighten
(titan)
whiten

3
enlighten
retighten

iter (īt′ər)

2
fighter
biter
lighter
slighter
miter
righter
(writer)
brighter
tighter
whiter
triter

3
indicter
bullfighter
delighter
politer

lamplighter
igniter
rewriter
typewriter
exciter

itest (īt′ĭst)

2
lightest
slightest
rightest
brightest
tritest
tightest
whitest

iteful (īt′fəl)

2
spiteful
rightful
frightful

ity (īt′ē)

2
mighty
nightie

iting (īt′ĭng)

2
biting
fighting
lighting
slighting
spiting
righting
(writing)
sighting
(citing)

3
indicting
cockfighting

bullfighting
delighting
handwriting
reciting
exciting
inviting
requiting
inciting
uniting
spotlighting
rewriting

itel (īt′l)

2
title
vital

3
recital
entitle
mistitle
requital
subtitle
retitle

iteless (īt′lĭs)

2
lightless
nightless
spiteless
rightless
sightless

itely (īt′lē)

2
lightly
slightly
nightly
rightly
brightly
tritely
tightly

3
politely
uprightly
contritely
unsightly

itement (īt′mənt)

3
indictment
incitement
excitement

iteness (īt′nĭs)

2
lightness
slightness
rightness
tightness
triteness
whiteness
brightness

itening (īt′nĭng)

2
heightening
lightning
tightening
brightening
frightening
whitening

ival (īv′əl)

3
revival
arrival
survival

iver (īv′ər)

2
diver
fiver

jiver
driver
striver

3
pearl diver
slave driver
contriver
survivor

**iving
(īv′ĭng)**

2
diving
jiving

driving
striving
thriving

3
conniving
arriving
contriving
reviving
surviving

izer (īz′ər)

2
geyser
Kaiser

miser
visor
wiser

3
incisor
baptizer
chastiser
advisor

**ising
(īz′ĭng)**

2
rising
sizing

3
surmising
despising
arrising
comprising
surprising
disguising
uprising
chastising

Triple eye (ī) sounds

When ladies still had propriety
Women like me were covered with glory.
But now since these damned society
Women invaded by territory. . . .

—*"Cocotte," lyric and music by Cole Porter*

iable
(ī′əbəl)

3 ———————
liable
pliable
viable

ieting
(ī′ətĭng)

3 ———————
dieting
rioting
quieting

icier (īs′ēər)

3 ———————
icier
spicier

iciest
(īs′ēĭst)

3 ———————
iciest
spiciest

itable
(īt′əbəl)

3 ———————
lightable
sightable
(citable)
fightable

ieter (ī′ətər)

3 ———————
dieter
rioter
quieter

ilander
(īl′əndər)

3 ———————
islander
highlander

icicle
(īs′ĭkəl)

3 ———————
icicle
bicycle
tricycle

itefully
(īt′fəlē)

3 ———————
spitefully
rightfully
frightfully

93

Single i (ĭ) sounds

Though you hush your lips,
Your finger tips
Tell me what I want to know.

—*"Hands Across the Table," lyric by Mitchell Parish,*
music by Jean DeLettre

ib (ĭb)

1
bib
fib
lib
glib
nib
rib
crib

ibbed (ĭbd)

1
fibbed
ribbed
cribbed

itch (ĭch)

1
itch
ditch
hitch
snitch
pitch
rich
stitch
witch
(which)
switch
twitch
bitch

2
unhitch
enrich
chain stitch
bewitch

itched (ĭcht)

1
itched
hitched
snitched
pitched
stitched
switched
twitched
bitched

2
unhitched
enriched
restitched
bewitched

id (ĭd)

1
id
bid
did

kid
skid
lid
slid
grid
quid
squid
Sid

2
forbid
outbid
undid
eyelid
amid
Madrid

3
underbid
overbid
overdid
invalid
pyramid
katydid

if (ĭf)

1
if
cliff

sniff
riff
stiff
whiff
skiff
tiff
miff

3
handkerchief
neckerchief

ift (ĭft)

1
gift
lift
miffed
sniffed
drift
thrift
shift
swift
whiffed

2
uplift
snowdrift
spendthrift

94

makeshift
gearshift

ig (ĭg)

1

big
dig
fig
gig
jig
pig
wig
twig
swig
rig

igged (ĭgd)

1

rigged
swigged
jigged

idge (ĭj)

1

midge
ridge
bridge

2

abridge
cabbage
cribbage
bondage
yardage
package
leakage
carnage
storage
dosage
message
sausage
usage
shortage

hostage
postage
language
voyage

3

appendage
foliage
cartilage
pilgrimage
patronage
brokerage
average
beverage
leverage
anchorage
heritage

ick (ĭk)

1

chick
Dick
hick
kick
lick
flick
click
slick
nick
pick
Rick
brick
crick
trick
sick
(sic)
tick
(tic)
stick
thick
Vic
wick
quick
prick

2

toothpick
firebrick
seasick
homesick
heartsick
lovesick
broomstick
drumstick
chopstick
Catholic

3

arsenic
limerick
maverick
rhetoric
lunatic
heretic
politic
walking stick
candlestick
candlewick

ix (ĭks)

1

fix
mix
nix
pix
(picks)
six
(sics)
tricks
chicks
hicks
kicks
licks
flicks
slicks
bricks
ticks
(tics)
sticks

wicks
pricks

2

affix
prefix
suffix
matchsticks

3

crucifix
intermix

ixed (ĭkst)

1

fixed
mixed
nixed

2

affixed
betwixt

icked (ĭkt)

1

kicked
licked
clicked
picked
bricked
tricked
strict
pricked
flicked
hicked
ticked

2

addict
predict
conflict
depict
restrict
constrict
evict
convict

3

contradict
Benedict

ill (il)

1

ill
bill
chill
dill
fill
(Phil)
gill
hill
Jill
kill
skill
mill
pill
spill
drill
frill
grill
shrill
till
still
will
quill
swill
twill
shill
sill
pill

2

playbill
refill
fulfill
bluegill
molehill
downhill
uphill
anthill
treadmill
windmill

quadrille
until
standstill
distill
Seville
good will
ill will
Brazil
instill

3

dollar bill
daffodil
chlorophyll
windowsill
volatile
whippoorwill

illed (ild)

1

gild
(guild)
billed
(build)
filled
milled
tilled
chilled
skilled
killed
willed
spilled
drilled
frilled
swilled
grilled
stilled

2

rebuild
refilled
unfilled
fulfilled
unskilled
distilled
instilled

strong-willed
weak-willed

ilk (ilk)

1

ilk
milk
bilk
silk

ilt (ilt)

1

built
gilt
(guilt)
jilt
spilt
wilt
quilt
silt
tilt
kilt
stilt
lilt

im (im)

1

dim
him
(hymn)
gym
(Jim)
Kim
skim
limb
slim
rim
grim
brim
trim
Tim
vim
swim
whim

3

cherubim
pseudonym
synonym
antonym
interim
homonym

immed (imd)

1

dimmed
skimmed
rimmed
brimmed
trimmed
slimmed

imf (imf)

1

lymph
nymph

imp (imp)

1

imp
skimp
limp
blimp
crimp
shrimp
pimp
gimp
primp

imps (imps)

1

glimpse
imps
limps
blimps

crimps
pimps
shrimps
primps
skimps

in (ĭn)

1

in
(inn)
bin
(been)
chin
din
fin
(Finn)
gin
kin
skin
Lynn
pin
spin
grin
sin
shin
thin
win
twin

2

herein
therein
wherein
within
robin
has-been
urchin
dolphin
begin
napkin
sheepskin
bearskin
muffin
Franklin

Kremlin
Berlin
Lenin
pippin
kingpin
pushpin
hatpin
chagrin
Latin
penguin
Catherine

3

paraffin
Mickey Finn
origin
alkaline
crystalline
zeppelin
javelin
mandolin
violin
Caroline
tarpaulin
insulin
discipline
masculine
Benjamin
vitamin
feminine
heroin
(heroine)
margarine
aspirin
glycerin
moccasin
Wisconsin
mortal sin
bulletin
intestine
thick and thin
harlequin
mannequin
genuine
saccharin

inch (ĭnch)

1

inch
finch
lynch
flinch
clinch
pinch
winch
cinch

inched (ĭncht)

1

inched
lynched
flinched
clinched
pinched
cinched

inned (ĭnd)

1

pinned
grinned
sinned
wind
spinned
skinned
thinned

2

thick-skinned
thin-skinned
rescind
whirlwind

ing (ĭng)

1

Bing
ding
king
fling
cling

Ming
ping
ring
bring
spring
string
sing
sting
thing
wing
swing
zing
sling

2

fledgling
changeling
weakling
offspring
mainspring
hamstring
shoestring
Sing Sing
something
nothing
evening
earring

3

foraging
pillaging
trafficking
rivaling
maddening
widening
deafening
toughening
strengthening
thickening
sickening
opening
happening
threatening
sweetening
softening
fastening

hastening
moistening
fattening
rationing
auctioning
questioning
echoing
murdering
suffering
angering
weathering
hollering
answering
motoring
featuring
fracturing
lecturing
picturing
purchasing
menacing
financing
promising
witnessing
publishing
ravishing
coveting
limiting
balloting
anything
everything
arguing
issuing
swallowing
lobbying
volleying
copying
varying

inge (ĭnj)

1 ───────
binge
hinge
fringe
cringe

twinge
singe
tinge

2 ───────
unhinge
infringe
syringe

ink (ĭngk)

1 ───────
ink
(Inc.)
think
fink
link
mink
pink
brink
drink
stink
shrink
wink
zinc
slink
sink
blink

2 ───────
unlink
hoodwink

inx (ĭngks)

1 ───────
sphinx
jinx
lynx
(links)
inks
thinks
finks
minx
(minks)
drinks
stinks

sinks
slinks
shrinks
winks
blinks

**inked
(ĭngkt)**

1 ───────
inked
linked
blinked
winked

ince (ĭns)

1 ───────
since
prince
wince
mince
rinse

2 ───────
evince
convince

int (ĭnt)

1 ───────
lint
hint
flint
splint
glint
mint
print
sprint
tint
squint
stint

2 ───────
skinflint
spearmint
reprint

hoofprint
imprint
misprint
footprint
blueprint
newsprint
pawprint

3 ───────
peppermint

ip (ĭp)

1 ───────
ship
dip
hip
skip
lip
flip
clip
slip
nip
snip
pip
rip
drip
grip
(grippe)
trip
strip
sip
tip
quip
whip
yip
zip
chip

2 ───────
harelip
catnip
outstrip
friendship
hardship

warship
flagship
kinship
township
airship
worship
courtship
equip
horsewhip

3

battleship
workmanship
penmanship
horsemanship
sportsmanship
fellowship
scholarship
membership
leadership
partnership

ipped (ĭpt)

1

chipped
skipped
dripped
slipped
crypt
script
whipped
dipped
shipped
flipped
clipped
nipped
snipped
ripped
gripped
tripped
stripped
sipped
tipped
quipped
zipped

2

subscript
transcript
conscript
postscript
horsewhipped
equipped
outstripped
worshipped

3

manuscript
superscript

iss (ĭs)

1

kiss
bliss
miss
Chris
sis
this
Swiss

2

remiss
dismiss

3

cowardice
prejudice
edifice
orifice
reminisce
licorice
Beatrice
emphasis
synthesis
nemesis
genesis

ish (ĭsh)

1

dish
fish

wish
squish
swish

2

crayfish
goldfish
swordfish
kingfish
dogfish
blackfish
shellfish
tilefish
crawfish
starfish
catfish
bluefish
anguish
selfish

3

jellyfish
devilish
yellowish
feverish

isk (ĭsk)

1

bisque
disk
(disc)
risk
brisk
frisk
whisk

3

obelisk
asterisk

isp (ĭsp)

1

lisp
crisp
wisp

ist (ĭst)

1

fist
kissed
list
mist
(missed)
wrist
tryst
cyst
twist
whist

2

enlist
dismissed
assist
subsist
resist
insist
consist
exist
persist
untwist

3

Methodist
athiest
pacifist
strategist
anarchist
specialist
socialist
analyst
catalyst
journalist
moralist
fatalist
novelist
pessimist
optimist
organist
botanist
columnist
Zionist

communist
Taoist
soloist
Eucharist
humorist
terrorist
motorist
publicist
exorcist
egotist
hypnotist
activist
pre-exist
hobbyist
lobbyist

it (ĭt)

1
it
bit
fit
hit
kit
skit
lit
split
slit
knit
pit
spit
grit
wit
quit

2
tidbit
unfit
misfit
outfit
moonlit
sunlit
submit
admit
emit
remit
commit
omit
transmit
cockpit
armpit
outwit
acquit

3
counterfeit
definite
infinite
hypocrite
favorite
opposite
exquisite
requisite
Jesuit

ith (ĭth)

1
myth
smith
pith

2
goldsmith
locksmith
gunsmith
herewith
therewith
forthwith

3
coppersmith
silversmith
metalsmith

iv (ĭv)

1
give
live
sieve

2
forgive
relive
outlive

3
combative
negative
sedative
talkative
narrative
expletive

iz (ĭz)

1
is
biz
fizz
his
Liz
quiz
whiz

izm (ĭz'əm)

2
schism
chrism
prism

3
theism
deism

4
atheism
pacifism
catechism
socialism
journalism
cataclysm
criticism
skepticism
mysticism
dogmatism
egotism
hypnotism
nepotism

Double i (ĭ) sounds

Oh, but your lips were thrilling,
Much too thrilling.
Never before were mine so
Strangely willing.

—*"Heart And Soul," lyric by Frank Loesser, music by*
Hoagy Carmichael

ibbit (ĭb′ĭt)

3 ——————
inhibit
prohibit
exhibit

**ibbing
(ĭb′ĭng)**

2 ——————
fibbing
ribbing

ibble (ĭb′əl)

2 ——————
nibble
dribble
scribble
sibyl
quibble

**ibbled
(ĭb′əld)**

2 ——————
ribald
dribbled
scribbled
quibbled
nibbled

**ibbler
(ĭb′lər)**

2 ——————
nibbler
dribbler
scribbler
quibbler

**ibbling
(ĭb′lĭng)**

2 ——————
nibbling
dribbling
scribbling
sibling
quibbling

**ibute
(ĭb′yo͞ot)**

3 ——————
attribute
contribute
distribute

**itcher
(ĭch′ər)**

2 ——————
snitcher
pitcher
richer
stitcher
switcher
twitcher

**itches
(ĭch′ĭz)**

2 ——————
itches
hitches
pitches
niches
snitches
riches
ditches
britches
witches
switches
twitches
stitches
bitches

itchy (ĭch′ē)

2 ——————
itchy
twitchy

**itching
(ĭch′ĭng)**

2 ——————
itching
ditching
hitching
pitching
stitching
switching
twitching

**itchless
(ĭch′lĭs)**

2 ——————
itchless
hitchless
stitchless

**idded
(ĭd′ĭd)**

2 ——————
kidded
skidded

**idden
(ĭd′n)**

2 ——————
hidden
ridden

**idding
(ĭd′ĭng)**

2 ——————
bidding
kidding
skidding

iddel (ĭd′l)

2

fiddle
middle
riddle
piddle
twiddle

iddler (ĭd′lər)

2

fiddler
riddler

iddling (ĭd′lĭng)

2

fiddling
piddling
twiddling
middling
riddling

idny (ĭd′nē)

2

kidney
Sydney
(Sidney)

iddo (ĭd′ō)

2

widow
kiddo

iffer (ĭf′ər)

2

differ
sniffer
stiffer

iffy (ĭf′ē)

2

iffy
jiffy
spiffy

ific (ĭf′ĭk)

3

prolific
terrific
Pacific
specific

iffle (ĭf′əl)

2

sniffle
whiffle

iffling (ĭf′lĭng)

2

sniffling
whiffling

ifted (ĭf′təd)

2

gifted
lifted
rifted
sifted
shifted

ifter (ĭf′tər)

2

drifter
swifter
snifter
sifter

ifty (ĭf′tē)

2

fifty
nifty
thrifty
shifty

ifting (ĭf′tĭng)

2

lifting
drifting
sifting
shifting
rifting

iftless (ĭft′lĭs)

2

giftless
thriftless
shiftless
riftless

igger (ig′ər)

2

bigger
jigger
rigger
(rigor)
trigger
vigor

3

gold digger
gravedigger
outrigger
square-rigger

iggy (ĭg′ē)

2

piggy
twiggy

igging (ĭg′ĭng)

2

digging
jigging
rigging
swigging

iggle (ĭg′əl)

2

giggle
jiggle
wriggle
wiggle
squiggle

iggler (ĭg′lər)

2

giggler
jiggler
wiggler
wriggler

iglet (ĭg′lĭt)

2

piglet
wiglet

iggly (ĭg′lē)

2

wiggly
squiggly
wriggly
giggly

iggling (ĭg′lĭng)

2

giggling
wiggling
jiggling
wriggling

igment (ĭg′mənt)

2

figment
pigment

ignant (ĭg′nənt)

3

indignant
malignant

iggit (ĭg′ĭt)

2

bigot
frigate

igure (ĭg′yər)

3

disfigure
transfigure

idget (ĭj′ĭt)

2

fidget
midget
Bridget
digit
widget

idgid (ĭj′ĭd)

2

rigid
frigid

idgen (ĭj′ən)

2

smidgen
pigeon

3

religion
stool pigeon

icken (ĭk′ən)

2

chicken
stricken
thicken
quicken

icker (ĭk′ər)

2

thicker
bicker
dicker
kicker
liquor
slicker
snicker
picker
tricker
sicker
vicar
wicker
quicker

ickest (ĭk′ĭst)

2

sickest
thickest
quickest

icket (ĭk′ĭt)

2

picket
cricket
wicket

ickets (ĭk′ĭts)

2

pickets
rickets
crickets
wickets

icky (ĭk′ē)

2

hickey
Mickey
picky
tricky
sticky
Vicky
Ricky
(rickey)

icking (ĭk′ĭng)

2

kicking
licking
flicking
clicking
nicking
picking
tricking
ticking
pricking
siccing

ickish (ĭk′ĭsh)

2

sickish
thickish
slickish

ickle (ĭk′əl)

2

fickle
nickel
pickle
trickle
tickle

ickler (ĭk′lər)

2

pickler
tickler
stickler
fickler

ickly (ĭk′lē)

2

thickly
quickly
prickly

ickling (ĭk′lĭng)

2

tickling
prickling
trickling

ickness (ĭk′nĭs)

2

sickness
thickness
quickness

103

ixer (ĭk′sər)

2 ───────
fixer
mixer

ikshun (ĭk′shən)

2 ───────
diction
fiction
friction

3 ───────
addiction
prediction
restriction
constriction
eviction
conviction
affliction
depiction

ixie (ĭk′sē)

2 ───────
Dixie
pixy
Trixie

ixing (ĭk′sĭng)

2 ───────
fixing
mixing
nixing

3 ───────
affixing

ixture (ĭks′chər)

2 ───────
fixture
mixture

icted (ĭk′təd)

3 ───────
addicted
predicted
afflicted
restricted
evicted
convicted
constricted

ictor (ĭk′tər)

2 ───────
victor

3 ───────
predictor
constrictor
evictor

icting (ĭk′tĭng)

3 ───────
addicting
predicting
inflicting
conflicting
depicting
restricting
constricting
evicting
convicting

ictive (ĭk′tĭv)

3 ───────
addictive
predictive
restrictive
constrictive

ickup (ĭk′ŭp)

2 ───────
hiccup
pickup

illa (ĭl′ə)

3 ───────
Manila
vanilla
guerrilla
(gorilla)
Priscilla
flotilla

illder (ĭl′dər)

3 ───────
rebuilder
shipbuilder
housebuilder
bewilder

illdoo (ĭl′dōō)

2 ───────
mildew
will do

iller (ĭl′ər)

2 ───────
chiller
killer
miller
pillar
driller
thriller
stiller
tiller

3 ───────
painkiller
man-killer
distiller

illful (ĭl′fəl)

2 ───────
skillful
willful

illy (ĭl′ē)

2 ───────
Billy
chilly
(chili)
(Chile)
hilly
lily
Millie
frilly
silly
Tillie
Willy

illage (ĭl′ĭj)

2 ───────
pillage
village

illing (ĭl′ĭng)

2 ───────
billing
chilling
filling
killing
spilling
drilling
grilling
thrilling
shilling
stilling
willing
swilling
tilling

3

fulfilling
distilling
instilling
unwilling

ilky (ĭl'kē)

2

silky
milky

**illness
(ĭl'nĭs)**

2

illness
stillness

illow (ĭl'ō)

2

billow
pillow
willow

**ilted
(ĭl'təd)**

2

jilted
lilted
wilted
quilted
silted
stilted
tilted

ilter (ĭl'tər)

2

filter
kilter

**ilting
(ĭl'tĭng)**

2

jilting
lilting

tilting
wilting
quilting
silting
stilting

**illyun
(ĭl'yən)**

2

billion
million
trillion

3

vermilion
cotillion
pavilion
civilian

**image
(ĭm'ĭj)**

2

image
scrimmage

**imbal
(ĭm'bəl)**

2

cymbal
(symbol)
timbal
(timbale)
thimble

**imber
(ĭm'bər)**

2

limber
timber
(timbre)

**immer
(ĭm'ər)**

2

dimmer
skimmer
glimmer
slimmer
primmer
trimmer
simmer
shimmer
swimmer

**immest
(ĭm'əst)**

2

dimmest
slimmest
trimmest
primmest

**immy
(ĭm'ē)**

2

jimmy
shimmy
gimme

**immick
(ĭm'ĭk)**

2

gimmick
mimic

**imming
(ĭm'ĭng)**

2

dimming
skimming
slimming
trimming
swimming

**imless
(ĭm'lĭs)**

2

limbless
rimless

**imper
(ĭm'pər)**

2

whimper
limper
crimper
simper

**impy
(ĭm'pē)**

2

skimpy
shrimpy

**imping
(ĭm'pĭng)**

2

skimping
limping
crimping
pimping
primping

**imple
(ĭm'pəl)**

2

dimple
pimple
simple

**imsy
(ĭm'zē)**

2

flimsy
whimsy

inching
(ĭn′chĭng)

2
inching
lynching
flinching
clinching
pinching
cinching

inder
(ĭn′dər)

2
hinder
cinder
tinder

indy (ĭn′dē)

2
lindy
Cindy
windy
Mindy

indle
(ĭnd′l)

2
kindle
spindle
swindle
dwindle

indling
(ĭnd′lĭng)

2
kindling
dwindling
swindling
spindling

inner
(ĭn′ər)

2
inner
dinner
skinner
spinner
thinner
sinner
winner

3
beginner
breadwinner

inger
(ĭng′ər)

2
slinger
ringer
(wringer)
springer
singer
stinger
swinger
clinger
stringer

3
humdinger
left-winger
right-winger
gunslinger

inging
(ĭng′ĭng)

2
flinging
clinging
ringing
(wringing)
bringing
springing
singing
stringing

stinging
winging
swinging

ingle
(ĭng′gəl)

2
jingle
mingle
single
tingle

ingless
(ĭng′lĭs)

2
ringless
wingless
stingless

ingling
(ĭng′lĭng)

2
mingling
tingling
jingling

inny (ĭn′ē)

2
Ginny
guinea
skinny
Minnie
tinny
Vinnie
whinny
(Winnie)

inning
(ĭn′ĭng)

2
inning
chinning
skinning

pinning
grinning
winning
sinning
spinning
thinning

injure
(ĭn′jər)

2
injure
ginger

injes
(ĭn′jĭz)

2
hinges
cringes
fringes
tinges
twinges
singes
binges

3
unhinges
infringes

injy (ĭn′jē)

2
dingy
stingy

injing
(ĭn′jĭng)

2
hinging
cringing
binging
fringing
tingeing
twinging
singeing

3

unhinging
infringing

**inker
(ĭng′kər)**

2

blinker
pinker
drinker
tinker
stinker
thinker
winker
sinker

**inky
(ĭng′kē)**

2

inky
kinky
pinkie
stinky

**inkage
(ĭng′kĭj)**

2

linkage
shrinkage

**inking
(ĭng′kĭng)**

2

linking
blinking
drinking
shrinking
thinking
stinking
winking
sinking

**inkle
(ĭng′kəl)**

2

wrinkle
crinkle
sprinkle
tinkle

**inkler
(ĭngk′lər)**

2

sprinkler
twinkler

**inkling
(ĭngk′lĭng)**

2

inkling
sprinkling
twinkling

**inctive
(ĭngk′tĭv)**

3

instinctive
distinctive

**inctly
(ĭngkt′lē)**

3

distinctly
succinctly

**inland
(ĭn′lənd)**

2

inland
Finland

**inless
(ĭn′lĭs)**

2

skinless
sinless

**incing
(ĭn′sĭng)**

2

rinsing
wincing
mincing

3

evincing
convincing

**inted
(ĭn′təd)**

2

hinted
glinted
splinted
minted
printed
sprinted
tinted
squinted

3

reprinted
imprinted
misprinted

**inter
(ĭn′tər)**

2

splinter
printer
sprinter
winter
squinter

3

midwinter

**inting
(ĭn′tĭng)**

2

hinting
minting
printing
sprinting
tinting
squinting
glinting

**ipper
(ĭp′ər)**

2

chipper
dipper
skipper
flipper
clipper
slipper
tripper
stripper
tipper
shipper
zipper
quipper

ippy (ĭp′ē)

2

dippy
nippy
hippie
snippy

**ipping
(ĭp′ĭng)**

2

chipping
dipping
skipping
clipping
nipping
slipping

snipping
whipping
ripping
gripping
stripping
sipping
shipping
tipping
quipping
whipping
zipping

3
outstripping
equipping
horsewhipping
unzipping

ipple (ĭp'əl)

2
nipple
ripple
triple
stipple

ipment (ĭp'mənt)

3
equipment
transshipment

ipshun (ĭp'shən)

3
Egyptian
subscription
description
prescription
transcription
inscription

ipsy (ĭp'sē)

2
Gypsy
tipsy

iptiv (ĭp'tĭv)

3
descriptive
prescriptive

issen (ĭs'ən)

2
glisten
christen
listen

issel (ĭs'əl)

2
missal
(missile)
bristle
gristle
thistle
whistle

issening (ĭs'ənĭng)

3
listening
glistening
christening

ishul (ĭsh'əl)

3
judicial
official
initial

ishun (ĭsh'ən)

2
fission
mission

3
magician
technician
patrician
optician
physician
musician
petition
admission
remission
omission
commission
position
partition
ambition
addition
tradition
edition
condition
audition
submission
emission
permission
transmission
ignition
cognition
munition
suspicion
contrition
nutrition

tactician
tuition
transition

ishent (ĭsh'ənt)

3
efficient
proficient
sufficient

isher (ĭsh'ər)

2
fisher
(fissure)
wisher

3
kingfisher
well-wisher

ishful (ĭsh'fəl)

2
dishful
wishful

ishing (ĭsh'ĭng)

2
dishing
fishing
wishing
swishing

ishyoo (ĭsh'oō)

2
issue
tissue

**ishus
(ĭsh'əs)**

2
vicious

3
ambitious
judicious
malicious
delicious
suspicious
auspicious
nutritious
fictitious

**issing
(ĭs'ĭng)**

2
hissing
kissing
missing

issit (ĭs'ĭt)

3
elicit
illicit
solicit
implicit
explicit

**issive
(ĭs'ĭv)**

3
submissive
omissive
permissive

isky (ĭs'kē)

2
risky
frisky
whiskey

**istence
(ĭs'təns)**

3
outdistance
assistance
resistance
existence
persistence
insistence
subsistence

**istent
(ĭs'tənt)**

3
assistant
resistant
existent
consistent
insistent
persistent

**isted
(ĭs'tĭd)**

2
listed
twisted
misted

3
tightfisted
close-fisted
two-fisted
enlisted
blacklisted
assisted
subsisted
resisted
insisted
consisted
existed
persisted
untwisted

ister (ĭs'tər)

2
blister
mister
sister
twister

3
sob sister
resister
stepsister

istic (ĭs'tĭk)

3
theistic
logistic
ballistic
stylistic
touristic
statistic
artistic
linguistic

**istics
(ĭs'tĭks)**

3
logistics
ballistics
statistics
linguistics

**isting
(ĭs'tĭng)**

2
listing
twisting
misting

3
enlisting
assisting
consisting
existing

resisting
subsisting
persisting
untwisting
blacklisting
insisting

itted (ĭt'ĭd)

2
knitted
fitted

3
unfitted
submitted
admitted
emitted
omitted
committed
transmitted
half-witted
acquitted
quick-witted
outwitted
dimwitted

itter (ĭt'ər)

2
bitter
litter
glitter
knitter
critter
sitter
quitter
titter

3
embitter
outfitter
pinch hitter
rail-splitter
transmitter

itty (ĭt′ē)

2

pity
gritty
pretty
city
witty

3

committee
self-pity

itting (ĭt′ĭng)

2

fitting
hitting
splitting
slitting
knitting
spitting
sitting
quitting

3

unwitting
remitting
admitting
acquitting
permitting
transmitting
omitting
emitting

ittish (ĭt′ĭsh)

2

skittish
British

ittle (ĭt′l)

2

little
brittle
whittle

3

remittal
transmittal
acquittal

itless (ĭt′lĭs)

2

pitless
witless
gritless

itten (ĭt′n)

2

kitten
mitten
smitten
Britain
(Briton)
written

3

flea-bitten
frostbitten
Great Britain
unwritten
rewritten

itness (ĭt′nĭs)

2

fitness
witness

ivven (ĭv′ən)

2

given
driven

ivver (ĭv′ər)

2

giver
liver
sliver
river
quiver

3

forgiver
deliver
upriver
downriver

ivvered (ĭv′ərd)

2

slivered
shivered
quivered

ivvid (ĭv′ĭd)

2

livid
vivid

ivving (ĭv′ĭng)

2

giving
living

3

lawgiving
forgiving

misgiving
thanksgiving
outliving

ivvel (ĭv′əl)

2

drivel
shrivel
civil
swivel

ivveling (ĭv′əlĭng)

3

sniveling
shriveling
swiveling
driveling

izzard (ĭz′ərd)

2

gizzard
blizzard
lizard
wizard

izhun (ĭzh′ən)

3

collision
decision
precision
incision
revision
provision
division
envision
derision

izzy (ĭz′ē)	izzing (ĭz′ĭng)	izzle (ĭz′əl)	izzen (ĭz′ən)
2		**2**	**3**
busy		chisel	arisen
dizzy	**2**	fizzle	imprison
Lizzie	quizzing	drizzle	
frizzy	fizzing	frizzle	
	frizzing	sizzle	
		swizzle	

111

Triple i (ĭ) sounds

Life is just a bowl of cherries,
Don't make it serious,
It's too mysterious.

—*"Life Is Just a Bowl of Cherries," music and lyric*
by Lew Brown and Ray Henderson

iftable
(ĭf′təbəl)

3 ——————
liftable
shiftable
siftable

ignify
(ĭg′nəfī)

3 ——————
signify
dignify

idgidly
(ĭj′ĭdlē)

3 ——————
rigidly
frigidly

ickening
(ĭk′ənĭng)

3 ——————
sickening
thickening
quickening

icketty
(ĭk′ĭtē)

3 ——————
rickety
crickety

ickory
(ĭk′ərē)

3 ——————
chicory
hickory

ixable
(ĭk′səbəl)

3 ——————
fixable
mixable

ikshunul
(ĭk′shənəl)

3 ——————
fictional
frictional

illable
(ĭl′əbəl)

3 ——————
fillable
killable
thrillable
syllable
tillable

illfully
(ĭl′fəlē)

3 ——————
skillfully
willfully

illiest
(ĭl′ēəst)

3 ——————
chilliest
hilliest
silliest

ilkiest
(ĭl′kēəst)

3 ——————
milkiest
silkiest

illowy
(ĭl′ōē)

3 ——————
billowy
willowy
pillowy

indicate
(ĭn′dĭkāt)

3 ——————
indicate
syndicate
vindicate

innical
(ĭn′ĭkəl)

3 ——————
cynical
clinical

112

innister
(ĭn′ĭstər)

3
minister
sinister

inkable
(ĭng′kəbəl)

3
drinkable
shrinkable
sinkable
thinkable

irical
(ĭr′əkəl)

3
lyrical
miracle

iskier
(ĭs′kēər)

3
riskier
friskier

iskiest
(ĭs′kēəst)

3
riskiest
friskiest

istery
(ĭs′tərē)

3
mystery
history

ittiest
(ĭt′ēəst)

3
prettiest
wittiest
grittiest

ittingly
(ĭt′ĭnglē)

3
fittingly
wittingly

ivvable
(ĭv′əbəl)

3
givable
livable

ivvery
(ĭv′ərē)

3
livery
shivery
quivery

ivvering
(ĭv′ərĭng)

3
shivering
quivering

izzier
(ĭz′ēər)

3
busier
dizzier

fizzier
frizzier

izziest
(ĭz′ēəst)

3
busiest
dizziest
fizziest
frizziest

izzical
(ĭz′ĭkəl)

3
physical
quizzical

izzily
(ĭz′əlē)

3
busily
dizzily

Single oh (ō) sounds

East is east and west is west,
And the wrong one I have chose,
Let's go where you'll keep on wearin' those
Frills and flowers and buttons and bows.

—*"Buttons and Bows," lyric and music by Jay*
  Livingston and Ray Evans

o (ō)

1
o
(oh)
(owe)

3
video
radio
rodeo
studio
Tokyo
folio
cameo
Romeo
Borneo
Scorpio
embryo
cheerio

bo (bō)

1
bo
(beau)
(bow)

2
rainbow
oboe
hobo
crossbow

doe (dō)

1
doe
(dough)

go (gō)

2
ago
forgo
outgo

3
touch and go
long ago
undergo
indigo
vertigo

ho (hō)

1
hoe

2
Soho
yo-ho

3
Idaho
Navaho
Westward ho!
Tallyho!

lo (lō)

1
low
blow
flow
glow
slow
(sloe)

2
pueblo
below
hello
ice floe
outflow
aglow
moonglow

3
buffalo
bungalow
counterblow
overflow
gigolo
tremolo

mo (mō)

1
mow

3
Alamo
Eskimo
dynamo

no (nō)

1
no
(know)
snow

ro (rō)

1
roe
(row)
grow
crow
pro
throw

2
hedgerow
outgrow
scarecrow
escrow
bureau

so (sō)

1
so
(sow)
(sew)

2
so-so
trousseau
also

117

toe (tō)

1
toe
(tow)
stow

2
plateau
chateau
tiptoe
bestow

oatch (ōch)

1
coach
poach
roach
broach
(brooch)

2
stagecoach
cockroach
encroach
approach
reproach

oatched (ōcht)

1
coached
poached
broached

2
encroached
approached
reproached

ode (ōd)

1
ode
(owed)

bode
goad
code
lode
(load)
slowed
mode
(mowed)
road
(rode)
(rowed)
crowed
sowed
(sewed)
towed
(toed)
(toad)
stowed
node
woad

2
abode
elbowed
forebode
unload
explode
commode
erode
corrode
bestowed

oaf (ōf)

1
oaf
loaf

oag (ōg)

1
rogue
brogue
vogue

oke (ōk)

1
oak
choke
folk
joke
coke
bloke
cloak
smoke
poke
spoke
broke
croak
stoke
stroke
soak
woke
yolk
(yoke)

2
kinfolk
townsfolk
baroque
sunstroke
evoke
revoke
invoke
provoke
awoke
heatstroke
convoke
uncloak
egg yolk
unyoke

oked (ōkt)

1
choked
joked
cloaked

smoked
poked
croaked
soaked
yoked

2
uncloaked
evoked
revoked
invoked
convoked
provoked
unyoked

ole (ōl)

1
bowl
dole
goal
hole
(whole)
coal
(kohl)
mole
poll
(pole)
roll
(role)
droll
scroll
troll
sole
(soul)
stroll
toll
stole
vole
shoal
foal

2
Creole
manhole

pinhole
loophole
porthole
cajole
charcoal
tadpole
maypole
flagpole
payroll
parole
enroll
insole
control
console
extoll
atoll

3 ───────
pigeonhole
buttonhole
casserole
self-control

old (ōld)

1 ───────
old
bold
(bowled)
fold
(foaled)
gold
hold
(holed)
cold
(coaled)
scold
mold
polled
(poled)
rolled
sold
(soled)
told
(tolled)
doled

2 ───────
blindfold
twofold
threefold
enfold
unfold
behold
freehold
stronghold
uphold
household
threshold
foothold
withhold
cajoled
remold
paroled
controlled
unsold
resoled
(resold)
retold
foretold

3 ───────
manifold
pigeonholed
uncontrolled
self-controlled
undersold
oversold

olt (ōlt)

1 ───────
bolt
jolt
colt
volt
dolt

2 ───────
rebolt
revolt

ome (ōm)

1 ───────
dome
foam
home
comb
Nome
(gnome)
roam
(Rome)
chrome
loam
tome

2 ───────
Jerome
afoam

3 ───────
catacomb
honeycomb
metronome
gastronome
hippodrome
chromosome

oan (ōn)

1 ───────
own
bone
phone
Joan
cone
scone
loan
(lone)
blown
moan
known
drone
groan
(grown)
prone
throne
(thrown)
sewn

(sown)
shown
(shone)
tone
stone
zone

2 ───────
disown
backbone
jawbone
wishbone
condone
alone
cologne
hormone
unknown
corn pone
postpone
half-grown
full-grown
dethrone
unsewn
(unsown)
atone
intone
limestone
sandstone
tombstone
ozone

3 ───────
anklebone
knucklebone
megaphone
dictaphone
telephone
xylophone
microphone
saxophone
chaperone
overgrown
baritone
monotone
overtone

119

cornerstone
overthrown

oned
(ōnd)

1

owned
boned
phoned
loaned
moaned
groaned
throned
toned
zoned

2

bemoaned
postponed
dethroned
atoned
intoned

ope (ōp)

1

dope
hope
cope
slope
mope
pope
rope
grope
soap
taupe
lope
nope

3

telescope
periscope
gyroscope
microscope
horoscope
stethoscope

cantaloupe
antelope
envelope
interlope
isotope

oped
(ōpt)

1

hoped
coped
sloped
moped
roped
soaped
groped

osse (ōs)

1

dose
close
gross

2

verbose
engross

3

overdose
grandiose
diagnose
comatose

oast (ōst)

1

boast
ghost
host
coast
most
post
roast
grossed
toast

2

seacoast
almost
utmost
signpost
outpost
foremost
engrossed

3

Southernmost
northernmost
innermost
uppermost
diagnosed
whipping
     post
hitching post

ote (ōt)

1

oat
boat
goat
coat
bloat
float
gloat
moat
(mote)
note
wrote
(rote)
throat
tote
vote
quote

2

lifeboat
sailboat
showboat
houseboat
scapegoat
redcoat

turncoat
topcoat
afloat
emote
demote
remote
promote
denote
keynote
footnote
rewrote
cutthroat
devote

3

ferryboat
riverboat
antidote
anecdote
billy goat
nanny goat
mountain
     goat
petticoat
overcoat

oath (ōth)

1

oath
both
sloth
growth

ove (ōv)

1

cove
rove
drove
stove
wove
grove

oves (ōvz)

1

cloves
loaves
droves
groves
stoves

oze (ōz)

1

owes
bows
chose
doze

foes
goes
glows
close
(clothes)
nose
(knows)
snows
rows
(rose)
froze
prose
(pros)
sows
(sews)

toes
(tows)
those

2

rainbows
bulldoze
enclose
foreclose
disclose
depose
repose
impose
compose
oppose

propose
expose
transpose
suppose
wild rose
primrose
tiptoes

3

dominoes
decompose
recompose
predispose
indispose
Irish rose

Double oh (ō) sounds

Even if we owe the grocer,
Don't we have fun?
Tax collector's getting closer,
Still we have fun.

—*"Ain't We Got Fun," lyric by Gus Kahn and*
Raymond Egan, music by Richard A. Whiting

oa (ō'ə)

2
Noah
boa

oaches (ōch'ĭz)

2
coaches
poaches
roaches
broaches
(brooches)

3
encroaches
approaches
cockroaches

oaching (ōch'ĭng)

2
coaching
poaching
broaching

oda (ōd'ə)

2
coda
Rhoda
soda

odal (ōd'l)

2
modal
yodel

oded (ōd'əd)

2
goaded
coded
loaded

oder (ōd'ər)

2
odor
goader
loader

3
reloader
unloader
exploder
corroder
freeloader

oding (ōd'ĭng)

2
coding
loading
goading

3
foreboding
decoding
unloading
exploding
eroding
corroding

ower (ō'ər)

2
ower
goer
lower
blower
glower
slower
mower
grower
sewer
(sower)

owest (ō'əst)

2
lowest
slowest

oafer (ōf'ər)

2
gopher
loafer
chauffeur

ogan (og'ən)

2
Logan
slogan

owy (ō'ē)

2
doughy
Joey
snowy
showy

owing (ō'ĭng)

2
owing
bowing
going
hoeing
glowing
slowing
mowing
knowing
snowing
rowing
growing
crowing
throwing
sowing
(sewing)
showing

122

towing
(toeing)
stowing

3

seagoing
foregoing
outgoing
unknowing
tiptoeing

okel (ōk′əl)

2

focal
local
vocal
yokel

**oken
(ōk′ən)**

2

spoken
broken
token

3

unspoken
well-spoken
soft-spoken
outspoken
unbroken
heartbroken

oker (ōk′ər)

2

ochre
choker
joker
smoker
poker
toker
stroker

3

stockbroker
revoker

invoker
provoker

okey (ōk′ē)

2

hokey
smoky
poky
(pokey)

**oking
(ōk′ĭng)**

2

choking
joking
cloaking
smoking
poking
croaking
stroking
soaking

3

evoking
revoking
invoking
provoking

**okless
(ōk′lĭs)**

2

jokeless
cloakless
smokeless
spokeless
yokeless
(yolkless)

oko (ōk′ō)

2

cocoa
poco
loco

**oaxing
(ōk′sĭng)**

2

hoaxing
coaxing

**okus
(ōk′əs)**

2

focus
hocus
locus

ola (ōl′ə)

3

Crayola
viola
Victrola

**olded
(ōl′dəd)**

2

folded
scolded
molded

3

blindfolded
unfolded
remolded

**olden
(ōl′dən)**

2

golden
olden

**older
(ōl′dər)**

2

older
bolder
(boulder)

holder
colder
smolder
shoulder

3

beholder
shareholder
cold shoulder

**oldest
(ōl′dəst)**

2

oldest
boldest
coldest

**olding
(ōl′dĭng)**

2

folding
holding
molding
scolding

3

enfolding
beholding
withholding
unfolding
remolding

oler (ōl′ər)

2

molar
polar
solar
stroller
roller
bowler

3

cajoler
patroller
controller
comptroller

oly (ōl'ē)

2

holy
(wholly)
solely

**oling
(ōl'ĭng)**

2

bowling
polling
rolling
strolling
trolling

3

controlling
paroling
consoling
extolling
patroling

olo (ōl'ō)

2

bolo
polo
solo

**olted
(ōl'təd)**

2

bolted
jolted
molted

3

unbolted
revolted

**olting
(ōl'tĭng)**

2

bolting
jolting
molting

3

unbolting
revolting

oma (ōm'ə)

2

coma
Roma

3

diploma
aroma

**omen
(ōm'ən)**

2

omen
yeoman

**oming
(ōm'ĭng)**

2

foaming
roaming
combing
gloaming
homing

**omeless
(ōm'lĭs)**

2

homeless
foamless
gnomeless
combless

**onent
(ōn'ənt)**

3

opponent
component
exponent

**oner
(ōn'ər)**

2

owner
donor
loaner
moaner
toner
boner

3

atoner
condoner
intoner

ony (ōn'ē)

2

pony
crony
bony
phony

**oning
(ōn'ĭng)**

2

owning
phoning
loaning
moaning
groaning
toning
zoning
honing

3

disowning
condoning
postponing
atoning

**oanless
(ōn'lĭs)**

2

boneless
phoneless
loanless
throneless
toneless
zoneless
stoneless

only (ōn'lē)

2

only
lonely

**onement
(ōn'mənt)**

3

postponement
atonement
intonement

**oping
(ōp'ĭng)**

2

hoping
coping
sloping
moping
roping
groping
soaping

**oapless
(ōp'lĭs)**

2

hopeless
soapless
popeless
ropeless

ora (ôr′ə)

2

Caura
Laura
Flora
Nora
torah

3

Pandora
señora

oral (ôr′əl)

2

oral
choral
floral

**orded
(ôr′dĭd)**

2

boarded
horded
(hoarded)

ory (ôr′ē)

2

gory
glory
story
hoary

**oring
(ôr′ĭng)**

2

boring
scoring
snoring
pouring
(poring)
roaring
soaring
storing

**oreless
(ôr′lĭs)**

2

doorless
scoreless
poreless
coreless
shoreless

**ornful
(ôrn′fəl)**

2

scornful
mournful

**orning
(ôr′nĭng)**

2

scorning
mourning
(morning)
warning

**oarsely
(ôrs′lē)**

2

hoarsely
coarsely

**orted
(ôr′tĭd)**

3

deported
reported
exported
transported
supported

**orter
(ôr′tər)**

3

reporter
exporter

supporter
transporter
deporter

**ortly
(ôrt′lē)**

2

courtly
portly
shortly

ocer (ōs′ər)

2

closer
grocer
(grosser)

**oshun
(ōsh′ən)**

2

ocean
lotion
motion
notion
potion

3

emotion
commotion
promotion
devotion

**oshus
(ōsh′əs)**

3

precocious
ferocious

osis (ōs′ĭs)

3

psychosis
osmosis
prognosis

hypnosis
neurosis

**osive
(ōs′ĭv)**

3

explosive
erosive
corrosive

**oastal
(ōst′l)**

2

coastal
postal

**oasted
(ōs′tĭd)**

2

hosted
roasted
toasted
boasted

**oasting
(ōs′tĭng)**

2

boasting
hosting
coasting
posting
roasting
toasting

**oted
(ōt′ĭd)**

2

floated
bloated
noted
voted
quoted

doted
coated

3
demoted
promoted
denoted
devoted
misquoted

oting
(ōt′ĭng)

2
boating
coating
floating
noting
voting
quoting
bloating
doting

3
promoting
devoting
denoting
misquoting

over (ōv′ər)

2
over
Dover
clover
rover

ozen
(ōz′ən)

2
chosen
frozen

ozer (ōz′ər)

3
bulldozer
forecloser

imposer
composer
opposer
exposer
supposer

ozes (ōz′ĭz)

2
dozes
closes
Moses
poses
roses
noses
hoses

ozhur
(ōzh′ər)

3
enclosure
disclosure
composure

exposure
foreclosure

ozhun
(ōzh′ən)

3
explosion
implosion
erosion
corrosion

ozing
(ōz′ĭng)

3
bulldozing
enclosing
deposing
imposing
composing
opposing
exposing
transposing

Single awe (ô) sounds

At last my heart's an open door,
And my secret love's no secret, anymore.

—"Secret Love," lyric by Paul Francis Webster,
music by Sammy Fain

aw (ô)

1
awe
jaw
law
flaw
claw
draw
straw
saw
thaw
caw
paw
maw

2
heehaw
coleslaw
withdraw
seesaw
foresaw

ob (ôb)

1
bob
gob
job
cob
blob
glob
slob
mob
knob
rob
snob
throb
sob
swab
hob
lob

2
corncob
hobnob

otch (ôtch)

1
scotch
blotch
botch
watch
swatch
notch
crotch

otched (ôtcht)

1
botched
blotched
watched

od (ôd)

1
odd
god
cod
clod
plod
nod
pod
rod
scrod
trod
sod
shod
squad
mod
Todd
bod

2
applaud
maraud
abroad
defraud

3
Ichabod
goldenrod

off (ôf)

1
cough
off
trough

oft (ôft)

2
coughed
loft
soft

ogg (ôg)

1
dog
fog
hog
jog
log
slog
clog
smog
frog
grog
cog

2
watchdog
bulldog
backlog
bullfrog

127

3

underdog
prairie dog
synagogue
dialogue
catalogue
monologue
polliwog

ogged (ôgd)

1

bogged
jogged
flogged
clogged

all (ôl)

1

all
ball
(bawl)
fall
gall
(Gaul)
hall
(haul)
call
moll
(maul)
small
pall
(Paul)
brawl
drawl
crawl
scrawl
sprawl
Saul
(Sol)
tall
stall
wall
squall
loll

shawl
doll

2

oddball
highball
blackball
pinball
snowball
baseball
football
catchall
windfall
rainfall
downfall
snowfall
nightfall
pitfall
dance hall
birdcall
recall
miscall
catcall
appall
Nepal
enthrall
install
sea wall
stonewall

3

all in all
free-for-all
basketball
Montreal
waterfall
alcohol
overhaul
protocol

alled (ôld)

1

bald
(bawled)
(balled)
galled

called
scald
drawled
crawled
mauled
stalled
sprawled

2

blackballed
snowballed
recalled
so-called
appalled
enthralled
stonewalled

alt (ôlt)

1

halt
fault
malt
salt
vault

2

cobalt
default
assault
exalt

on (ôn)

1

on
Don
John
gone
wan
swan

ong (ông)

1

gong
long
pong
strong

song
wrong
dong
tong
thong
throng
prong

2

ding-dong
Mah-Jongg
Hong Kong
along
headlong
belong
lifelong
prolong
Ping-Pong
sarong
headstrong
singsong

or (ôr)

1

or
(ore)
(oar)
(o'er)
bore
(boar)
door
for
(four)
(fore)
gore
core
(corps)
score
floor
more
snore
pour
(pore)
roar
soar

(sore)
shore
store
tore
wore
(war)
swore

2
adore
indoor
outdoor
before
therefore
wherefore
decor
folklore
deplore
explore
ignore
downpour
outpour
eyesore
ashore
seashore
restore
drugstore

3
troubadour
picador
matador
Isadore
stevedore
Theodore
commodore
two-by-four
pinafore
albacore
underscore
sycamore
Baltimore
sophomore
furthermore
evermore
nevermore

Singapore
carnivore
Labrador
meteor
Eleanor
promisor
dinosaur
tug of war
man-of-war

ortch (ôrch)

1
scorch
porch
torch

ord (ôrd)

1
bored
(board)
ford
gored
(gourd)
hoard
(horde)
floored
poured
(pored)
toward
sword
snored
ward
(warred)
lord
chord
(cored)

2
aboard
switchboard
headboard
sideboard
cardboard
seaboard

surfboard
springboard
blackboard
inboard
outboard
adored
two-doored
four-doored
afford
deplored
implored
explored
restored
landlord
award
reward
accord
abhorred

3
shuffleboard
overboard
open-doored
unexplored
harpsichord
clavichord
overlord
diving board

orm (ôrm)

1
dorm
form
norm
storm
warm
swarm

2
deform
reform
inform
conform
perform
transform

barnstorm
lukewarm

3
uniform
misinform
chloroform
thunderstorm

**ormed
(ôrmd)**

1
formed
stormed
warmed
swarmed

orn (ôrn)

1
born
scorn
mourn
(morn)
warn
(worn)
sworn
shorn
corn
torn
thorn
horn

2
reborn
freeborn
firstborn
newborn
adorn
longhorn
foghorn
French horn
greenhorn
shoehorn
popcorn
forlorn

lovelorn
midmorn
hawthorn
forewarn

orned
(ôrnd)

1

scorned
mourned
warned

orce (ôrs)

1

horse
(hoarse)
coarse
(course)
Morse
Norse
force

2

enforce
endorse
recourse
discourse
resource
divorce

3

reinforce
intercourse

ort (ôrt)

1

snort
sort
short
tort
wart
quart
thwart
court
port
fort
sport

2

deport
report
seaport
import
airport
carport
passport
export
transport
support
resort
abort
exhort
escort
assort
consort

retort
contort
distort
cavort

3

davenport
nonsupport

oss (ôs)

1

boss
loss
gloss
moss
cross
sauce
toss

2

emboss
across

ost (ôst)

1

cost
lost
frost
crossed
tossed

3

Pentecost
Holocaust
double-
crossed

oth (ôth)

1

cloth
moth
broth
froth
troth

2

broadcloth
oilcloth
loincloth
betroth

aws (ôz)

1

Oz
(awes)
gauze
cause
claws
(clause)
paws
(pause)

Double awe (ô) sounds

Seeing this night in its glory
You people so loyal, so true,
Puts me in mind of a story,
It might have happened to you.

—"The Waiter and the Porter and the Upstairs
Maid," words and music by Johnny Mercer

awded
(ôd'id)

3 ———
applauded
marauded
defrauded

awdel
(ôd'l)

2 ———
dawdle
caudle

offer (ôf'ər)

2 ———
offer
cougher
(coffer)
scoffer

offen
(ôf'ən)

2 ———
often
soften

awful
(ôf'əl)

2 ———
awful
lawful

awing
(ô'ĭng)

2 ———
jawing
gnawing
pawing
drawing
sawing

awker
(ôk'ər)

2 ———
balker
chalker
gawker
hawker

3 ———
jaywalker
sleepwalker
streetwalker
nightwalker

alding
(ôl'dĭng)

2 ———
balding
scalding

awless
(ôl'ĭs)

2 ———
lawless
flawless
jawless
pawless
clawless

allest
(ôl'ĭst)

2 ———
smallest
tallest

alling
(ôl'ĭng)

2 ———
balling
(bawling)
falling
hauling
calling
mauling

brawling
crawling
scrawling
stalling
squalling
sprawling
drawling

3 ———
blackballing
snowballing
recalling
appalling
enthralling
installing

alted
(ôl'tĭd)

2 ———
halted
salted
vaulted

alter (ôl'tər)

2 ———
alter
(altar)
falter
halter
vaulter
Walter

131

3
Gibraltar
assaulter
exalter

olving
(ŏl′vĭng)

3
absolving
resolving
dissolving
evolving
revolving
involving

awning
(ôn′ĭng)

2
awning
fawning
pawning
spawning
yawning

awnted
(ôn′tĭd)

2
daunted
haunted
flaunted
taunted
wanted

ortcherd
(ôr′chərd)

2
orchard
tortured

ortching
(ôr′chĭng)

2
scorching
torching

orded
(ôr′dĭd)

3
accorded
recorded
awarded
rewarded
afforded

ordered
(ôr′dərd)

2
ordered
bordered

ording
(ôr′dĭng)

3
according
awarding
rewarding
affording

orrence
(ôr′əns)

2
Lawrence
Florence

oric (ôr′ĭk)

3
caloric
historic
euphoric

ormal
(ôr′məl)

2
formal
normal

3
informal
abnormal

ormon
(ôr′mən)

2
Mormon
Norman

ormat
(ôr′măt)

2
doormat
format

ormer
(ôr′mər)

2
dormer
former
warmer

orming
(ôr′mĭng)

2
forming
warming
storming
swarming

3
reforming
informing
conforming
performing
transforming
brainstorming
barnstorming
housewarming

orny (ôr′nē)

2
horny
corny
thorny

orted
(ôr′tĭd)

3
exhorted
extorted
aborted
escorted
assorted
retorted
distorted
cavorted
resorted

orter
(ôr′tər)

2
mortar
quarter
sorter
shorter
porter

orting
(ôr′tĭng)

3
aborting
exhorting
consorting
distorting
cavorting
resorting
extorting
escorting
retorting

ossy (ôs′ē)

2
bossy
flossy
glossy
saucy

Single oo (o͝o) sounds

If they asked me I could write a book,
About the way you walk and whisper, and look.

—"I Could Write a Book," lyric by Lorenz
   Hart, music by Richard Rodgers

ood (o͝od)

1
good
hood
could
should
stood
wood
(would)

2
manhood
knighthood
withstood
redwood
deadwood
wildwood
dogwood
plywood
firewood
rosewood
driftwood
wormwood

ook (o͝ok)

1
book
cook
hook
look
rook
brook
crook
shook
took
nook

2
cookbook
unhook
fishhook
outlook
mistook

ool (o͝ol)

1
pull
full
wool

2
dreadful
gleeful
half-full
spoonful
watchful
bashful
wishful
mouthful
roomful
sinful
helpful
cupful
glassful
joyful
lambswool
grateful
hopeful

oosh (o͝osh)

2
rosebush
smoke bush

oot (o͝ot)

1
foot
put
soot

2
afoot
clubfoot
Blackfoot
barefoot

133

Double oo (o͝od) sounds

Lookie, lookie, lookie
Here comes cookie, gotta fix my tie.
Just a little angel, playin' hookie
From heaven on high.

—*"Here Comes Cookie," words and music by Mack*
  Gordon

ooded (o͝od'ĭd)	ooker (o͝ok'ər)	ooking (o͝ok'ĭng)	ully (o͝ol'ē)
2	2	2	2
hooded	hooker	booking	bully
wooded	booker	cooking	fully
	looker	looking	pulley
	snooker	hooking	woolly

Single oy (oi) sounds

Our traffic is so congested,
Mass confusion on wheels.
But Detroit
Is adroit
What they'll do in Detroit
Is make bigger automobiles.

—*"It's a Mad, Mad, Mad, Mad World," lyric by*
Mack David, music by Ernest Gold

oy (oi)

1
boy
(buoy)
foy
joy
coy
Roy
Troy
toy
ploy
soy

3
altar boy
overjoy
Illinois
corduroy
Iroquois

oid (oid)

1
buoyed
Lloyd
Floyd
Freud
toyed
void

2
enjoyed
decoyed
typhoid
alloyed
deployed
employed
tabloid
annoyed

3
overjoyed
alkaloid
unemployed
asteroid

oil (oil)

1
oil
boil
(Boyle)
foil
coil
spoil
soil
toil
broil

2
gargoyle
recoil

uncoil
turmoil
embroil

oiled (oild)

1
oiled
boiled
foiled
spoiled
broiled
soiled
toiled

oin (oin)

1
coin
loin
join
groin

2
adjoin
sirloin
Des Moines

oint (oint)

1
joint
point

2
disjoint
appoint
viewpoint
anoint

oice (ois)

1
choice
voice

2
rejoice
Rolls Royce
invoice

oist (oist)

1
hoist
moist
voiced
joist

2
rejoiced
invoiced

135

Double oy (oi) sounds

Down by the sea lived a lonesome oyster,
Every day getting sadder and moister.

—*"Tale of the Oyster," words and music by Cole Porter*

oyal (oi'əl)

2 ———————
loyal
royal

**oyant
(oi'ənt)**

3 ———————
flamboyant
clairvoyant

oyer (oi'ər)

3 ———————
employer
destroyer

**oying
(oi'ĭng)**

3 ———————
enjoying
deploying
employing
annoying
destroying

**oiler
(oil'ər)**

2 ———————
oiler
boiler
spoiler
broiler
soiler

toiler
foiler

**oiling
(oil'ĭng)**

2 ———————
oiling
boiling
foiling
spoiling
broiling
soiling
toiling

**ointed
(oin'təd)**

2 ———————
jointed
pointed

3 ———————
disjointed
appointed
anointed
pinpointed

**ointing
(oin'tĭng)**

2 ———————
jointing
pointing

3 ———————
disjointing
anointing
appointing
pinpointing

136

Single ow (ou) sounds

Once you've found him,
Build your world around him.

—*"Make Someone Happy," lyric by Betty Comden and*
Adolph Green, music by Jule Styne

ow (ou)

1
how
bow
cow
plow
now
vow
thou
wow
pow
row
sow

2
endow
somehow
allow
snowplow
eyebrow
highbrow
avow
bow-wow

3
anyhow
disallow
disavow

ouch (ouch)

1
ouch
couch
slouch
pouch
grouch
crouch
vouch

oud (oud)

1
loud
cloud
bowed
plowed
crowd
proud
shroud
vowed
wowed

2
endowed
allowed
(aloud)
avowed

owl (oul)

1
owl
fowl
(foul)
howl
jowl
scowl

growl
prowl

oun (oun)

1
down
clown
noun
brown
frown
crown
town

2
touchdown
rubdown
shakedown
sundown
lowdown
showdown
nightgown
renown
pronoun
downtown
uptown

ound (ound)

1
bound
found
hound

clowned
mound
pound
round
drowned
frowned
ground
crowned
sound
wound

2
rebound
spellbound
icebound
westbound
eastbound
outbound
inbound
northbound
southbound
dumbfound
confound
profound
greyhound
bloodhound
renowned
impound
compound
around
background
surround
astound

3

middle
ground
underground

**ounds
(oundz)**

1

hounds
pounds
grounds
sounds
mounds
rounds

**ounce
(ouns)**

1

ounce
bounce
pounce
trounce
flounce
jounce

2

announce
pronounce

renounce
denounce

ount (ount)

1

count
mount

2

account
recount
discount
amount
dismount

our (our)

1

our
(hour)
scour
flour
sour
dour

owse (ous)

1

house
blouse
mouse

grouse
souse
louse
douse
spouse

2

clubhouse
guardhouse
doghouse
storehouse
poorhouse
lighthouse
penthouse

out (out)

1

out
scout
clout
pout
spout
sprout
trout
shout
tout
stout
grout
route
lout

2

hangout
dugout
tryout
blackout
knockout
walkout
lookout
shutout
without
throughout
about
boy scout
devout

3

in-and-out
out-and-out
roundabout
thereabout
whereabout
knockabout
roustabout
waterspout

outh (outh)

1

mouth
south

Double ow (ou) sounds

We two should be like clams in a dish of chowder;
But we just "fizz" like parts of a Seidlitz powder.

—*"A Fine Romance," words by Dorothy Fields, music by Jerome Kern*

owded
(oud′ĭd)

2
clouded
crowded
shrouded

owder
(oud′ər)

2
chowder
louder
powder

3
clam chowder
gunpowder

owdy
(oud′ē)

2
howdy
cloudy
rowdy
dowdy

owwel
(ou′əl)

2
dowel
towel

vowel
trowel

owwer
(ou′ər)

2
dower
flower
plower
(plougher)
power
shower
tower
bower
cower

3
allower
wallflower
sunflower
Mayflower
horsepower
manpower
watchtower

owwing
(ou′ĭng)

2
ploughing
(plowing)
vowing

bowing
wowing

ounded
(oun′dĭd)

2
bounded
founded
hounded
pounded
grounded
sounded
rounded
mounded

3
rebounded
dumbfounded
unfounded
compounded
expounded
astounded

ounding
(oun′dĭng)

2
hounding
pounding
grounding
sounding
rounding
mounding

3
rebounding
confounding
compounding
resounding
surrounding
astounding
dumbfounding

ouncing
(oun′sĭng)

2
bouncing
flouncing
pouncing
trouncing
jouncing

3
announcing
renouncing
pronouncing

ouncement
(ouns′mənt)

3
announcement
pronouncement
renouncement

139

**ounty
(oun′tē)**

2 ——————

bounty
county
Mounty

**ountin
(oun′tən)**

2 ——————

fountain
mountain

**ounting
(oun′tĭng)**

2 ——————

counting
mounting

**ouring
(our′ĭng)**

2 ——————

scouring
flouring
souring

**outed
(out′ĭd)**

2 ——————

doubted
scouted
pouted
spouted
shouted

touted
routed
sprouted
grouted
clouted

**outer
(out′ər)**

2 ——————

outer
scouter
spouter
sprouter
touter
shouter
stouter

pouter
router
grouter

**outing
(out′ĭng)**

2 ——————

outing
doubting
scouting
pouting
routing
grouting
shouting
sprouting
clouting

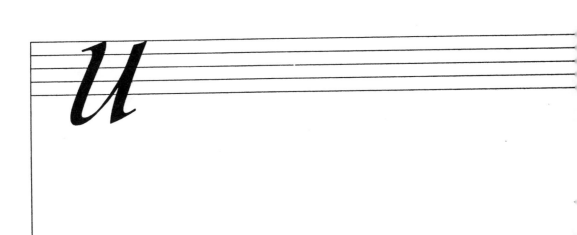

Single ou (ōō) sounds

You go to my head like a sip of sparkling Burgundy brew,
And I find the very mention of you,
Like the kicker in a julep or two.

—*"You Go To My Head," lyric by Haven Gillespie,*
music by J. Fred Coots

boo (bōō)

2 ─────────
taboo
bamboo

3 ─────────
peekaboo
marabou
caribou

doo (dōō)

1 ─────────
do
(due)
(dew)

2 ─────────
ado
(adieu)
subdue
redo
mildew
Perdue
outdo
hoodoo
to-do
voodoo

loo (lōō)

1 ─────────
Lou
(loo)
(lieu)

blue
(blew)
flu
(flew)
glue
clue
slew

2 ─────────
sky-blue
true-blue
igloo
lulu
Zulu

noo (nōō)

1 ─────────
new
(knew)
(gnu)

2 ─────────
canoe
renew

3 ─────────
ingénue
avenue
revenue

roo (rōō)

1 ─────────
rue
brew

drew
grew
crew
screw
true
threw
(through)

2 ─────────
withdrew
Peru
accrue
corkscrew
thumbscrew
unscrew
untrue

3 ─────────
kangaroo
buckaroo

too (tōō)

1 ─────────
to
(too)
(two)
stew

2 ─────────
tattoo
lean-to
hereto
thereto
tutu

whereto
unto
into

ooed (ōōd)

1 ─────────
booed
chewed
food
feud
lewd
glued
mood
nude
rude
brood
(brewed)
crude
screwed
prude
shrewd
shooed
stewed
viewed

2 ─────────
tabooed
unglued
allude
elude
prelude
preclude
seclude

143

include
conclude
exclude
renewed
shampooed
accrued
unscrewed
intrude
protrude
extrude
pursued
etude
reviewed
previewed

3
misconstrued
longitude
latitude
solitude
amplitude
magnitude
multitude
fortitude
gratitude
servitude

oodes (o͞odz)

1
foods
moods
nudes
broods

oof (o͞of)

1
goof
spoof
proof
roof

2
aloof
fireproof
foolproof

ouk (o͞ok)

1
uke
duke
Luke
fluke
spook
nuke
puke
souk

oul (o͞ol)

1
fool
ghoul
cool
mule
pool
spool
drool
tool
stool
Yule

2
whirlpool
slide rule
toadstool
footstool

3
vestibule
Istanbul
April fool
molecule
ridicule
Sunday
  school
swimming
  pool
wading pool
Liverpool
overrule

oom (o͞om)

1
boom
doom
loom
gloom
plume
room
broom
(brougham)
groom
tomb
womb
whom
zoom
flume

2
bedroom
tearoom
cloakroom
ballroom
storeroom
stateroom
courtroom
mushroom
bridegroom
assume
consume
entomb
costume
resume
presume
classroom
spare room
whiskbroom

oon (o͞on)

1
boon
(Boone)
dune
goon
June
moon
noon

spoon
croon
prune
strewn
soon
tune
swoon
loon

2
baboon
typhoon
buffoon
lagoon
tycoon
balloon
doubloon
immune
lampoon
harpoon
impugn
teaspoon
maroon
cartoon

3
honeymoon
harvest moon
tablespoon
macaroon
opportune

ooned
(o͞ond)

1
spooned
mooned
tuned
wound
swooned
crooned

oop (o͞op)

1
dupe
coop

(coupe)
scoop
loop
bloop
sloop
snoop
droop
group
troop
(troupe)
soup
stoop
swoop

ooped
(ōōped)

1
duped
cooped
looped
drooped
grouped
trooped
stooped
swooped

oor (ōōr)

1
moor
pure
poor
(pour)
sure
tour
your
(you're)

2
endure
secure
obscure
allure
amour
demure

impure
insure
ensure
unsure
mature
gravure

3
insecure
manicure
tablature
premature
immature
signature
curvature
forfeiture
furniture
aperture
overture

oored
(ōōrd)

2
secured
obscured
insured

ooce (ōōs)

1
juice
loose
use
moose
(mousse)
noose
Bruce
spruce
Zeus

2
abuse
reduce

seduce
induce
produce
diffuse
profuse
excuse
recluse
papoose
misuse
obtuse

3
reproduce
introduce
Syracuse
charlotte
    russe

oote (ōōt)

1
boot
hoot
cute
scoot
loot
(lute)
flute
mute
snoot
route
(root)
fruit
chute
(shoot)
suit

2
dilute
salute
pollute
commute
minute
dispute
breadfruit
recruit

lawsuit
pursuit
astute

3
attribute
convolute
persecute
absolute
execute
resolute
dissolute
evolute
parachute
substitute
institute
constitute
destitute

ooth (ōōth)

1
booth
sleuth
Ruth
tooth
youth
truth

2
forsooth
eyetooth

oove (ōōv)

1
move
groove
prove
you've

2
behoove
remove
approve
improve

145

disprove
reprove

ooved
(o͞ovd)

1 ————————
moved
proved
grooved
hooved

ooze (o͞oz)

1 ————————
ooze
use

booze
(boos)
choose
(chews)
dues
fuse
coos
blues
flues
clues
muse
(mews)
news
snooze
bruise
(brews)
cruise
(crews)

sues
lose
(loos)
stews
shoes
(shoos)
zoos

2 ————————
abuse
taboos
refuse
defuse
infuse
confuse
transfuse
accuse
excuse

amuse
canoes
shampoos
misuse
tattoos
horseshoes

oozed
(o͞ozd)

1 ————————
used
oozed
fused
snoozed
bruised
cruised

Double ou (o͞o) sounds

Ach! When I choose 'em,
I love a great boosom!

—"I Love Louisa," lyric by Howard Dietz, music
by Arthur Schwartz

oodest
(o͞od′ĭst)

2 ────────
nudest
(nudist)
rudest
crudest
shrewdest
feudist
Buddhist
lewdest

oodely
(o͞od′lē)

2 ────────
shrewdly
crudely
rudely

ooel (o͞o′əl)

2 ────────
duel
fuel
jewel
gruel
cruel
newel

ooer (o͞o′ər)

2 ────────
fewer
skewer

bluer
newer
sewer
viewer

ooey (o͞o′ē)

2 ────────
gooey
hooey
flooey
gluey
Huey
bowie
(buoy)
chewy
phooey
Louis
screwy

3 ────────
mildewy
St. Louis
chop suey

ooest
(o͞o′ĭst)

2 ────────
fewest
bluest

truest
newest

oofer
(o͞of′ər)

2 ────────
goofer
roofer
hoofer

oogle
(o͞og′əl)

2 ────────
fugal
frugal
bugle

ooing
(o͞o′ĭng)

2 ────────
booing
chewing
doing
cooing
gluing
brewing
shooing
strewing

3 ────────
subduing
undoing
misdoing
outdoing
rescuing
canoeing
renewing
shampooing
accruing
horseshoeing
tattooing
reviewing
previewing

ooler
(o͞ol′ər)

2 ────────
cooler
ruler
fooler
tooler
pooler
dueller

ooly (o͞ol′ē)

2 ────────
duly
newly
truly
coolly
(coolie)

147

ooling
(ōōl'ĭng)

2
fooling
cooling
schooling
pooling
spooling
ruling
drooling

ooman
(ōōm'ən)

2
human
crewman
Newman
Truman

oomer
(ōōm'ər)

2
boomer
humor
rumor
tumor

oomered
(ōōm'ərd)

2
humored
rumored

ooner
(ōōn'ər)

2
schooner
spooner
crooner
sooner
swooner
tuner
pruner

3
ballooner
sublunar
harpooner
marooner

oonful
(ōōn'fəl)

2
spoonful
tuneful

ooning
(ōōn'ĭng)

2
spooning
crooning
pruning
swooning

oonist
(ōōn'ĭst)

3
balloonist
lampoonist
bassoonist
cartoonist

ooper
(ōōp'ər)

2
duper
hooper
cooper
scooper
looper
grouper
trooper
(trouper)
super
stupor
swooper

ooping
(ōōp'ĭng)

2
looping
drooping
grouping
scooping
trooping
stooping
swooping

ooral
(ōōr'əl)

2
Ural
mural
plural
rural

ooror
(ōōr'ər)

2
führer
juror
purer
poorer

oorest
(ōōr'ĭst)

2
purest
poorest
surest

ooring
(ōōr'ĭng)

2
during
mooring
touring

3
enduring
securing
procuring
obscuring
alluring
assuring
insuring
maturing

oorly
(ōōr'lē)

2
poorly
purely
surely
dourly

3
securely
obscurely
demurely
impurely
maturely

ooshun
(ōōsh'ən)

3
pollution
dilution
solution

oosive
(ōōs'ĭv)

3
conducive
elusive
illusive
reclusive
inclusive
conclusive
intrusive
obtrusive
effusive

ooseless
(o͞os'lĭs)

2
useless
juiceless

oosome
(o͞os'əm)

2
gruesome
twosome

ooted
(o͞ot'əd)

2
looted
fluted
muted
rooted
fruited
suited
tooted

3
refuted
saluted
diluted
polluted
commuted
reputed
computed

uprooted
recruited

ooty (o͞ot'ē)

2
booty
beauty
duty
cutie
snooty
fruity
tutti

ooting
(o͞ot'ĭng)

2
looting
fluting
rooting
suiting
shooting
tooting

3
refuting
diluting
polluting
saluting
commuting
computing
recruiting

oover
(o͞ov'ər)

3
Vancouver
remover
approver
improver

oovie
(o͞ov'ē)

2
movie
groovy

oozer
(o͞oz'ər)

2
user
boozer
chooser
loser
bruiser
cruiser

oozes
(o͞oz'ĭz)

2
uses
chooses
fuses
snoozes

bruises
cruises

oozhun
(o͞ozh'ən)

3
diffusion
infusion
transfusion
allusion
delusion
illusion
collusion
seclusion
conclusion
exclusion
intrusion
protrusion

oozing
(o͞oz'ĭng)

2
oozing
boozing
choosing
fusing
losing
musing
snoozing
bruising
cruising

Single uh (ŭ) sounds

Except on Wednesday night, it's walk, don't run.
I just kill time till Mr. Kirkeby's done
With his Wednesday night fun!

—"Upstairs," lyric by Hal David, music by Burt
  Bacharach

ub (ŭb)

1
cub
hub
flub
club
nub
snub
pub
rub
grub
scrub
sub
stub
tub

ubbed (ŭbd)

1
dubbed
clubbed
rubbed
scrubbed
stubbed
grubbed
subbed

utch (ŭch)

1
Dutch
hutch
clutch
much
crutch
such
touch

utched (ŭcht)

1
clutched
touched

ud (ŭd)

1
bud
flood
mud
spud
stud
thud

uff (ŭf)

1
buff
duff
guff
cuff
scuff
bluff
slough
snuff
ruff
(rough)
gruff
tough
(tuff)
stuff

2
rebuff
handcuff
enough
cream puff

ug (ŭg)

1
chug
bug
dug
hug
jug
lug
slug
mug
smug
rug
thug
tug

udge (ŭj)

1
fudge
judge
sludge
smudge
nudge
drudge
grudge
trudge

udged (ŭjd)

1
fudged
judged
smudged
trudged
nudged

uck (ŭk)

1
buck
chuck
duck
luck
cluck
pluck
truck
shuck
tuck
stuck

uct (ŭkt)

2
abduct
induct
conduct

obstruct
instruct
construct

ull (ŭl)

1

hull
skull
mull
dull
cull

ulk (ŭlk)

1

bulk
hulk
sulk

ult (ŭlt)

2

adult
occult
insult
consult
result
exult

um (ŭm)

1

chum
dumb
gum
come
glum
plumb
rum
crumb
strum
some
(sum)

thumb
yum

2

kingdom
become
succumb
humdrum
threesome
wholesome
lonesome
awesome
gruesome
twosome
yumyum

3

tweedledum
Christendom
martyrdom
overcome
sodium
calcium
stadium
cadmium
lithium
platinum
troublesome
quarrelsome
meddlesome
cumbersome
bothersome

ump (ŭmp)

1

bump
chump
dump
hump
jump
lump
clump
slump
pump

rump
trump
crump
stump
thump

un (ŭn)

1

done
(dun)
fun
gun
Hun
(hon')
none
(nun)
pun
spun
run
sun
(son)
ton
stun
one
(won)

2

well-done
undone
outdone
begun
homespun
outrun
grandson

unch (ŭnch)

1

lunch
munch
punch
brunch
crunch

unned (ŭnd)

1

fund
shunned
sunned

unk (ŭngk)

1

dunk
funk
skunk
junk
clunk
plunk
monk
punk
drunk
trunk
sunk

unt (ŭnt)

1

bunt
hunt
blunt
punt
brunt
grunt
stunt

ur (ŭr)

1

fir
(fur)
her
blur
slur
per
(purr)
sir
spur

stir
were

2

defer
prefer
infer
confer
chauffeur
transfer
recur
concur
occur
liqueur
demur
Pasteur

3

caliber
caliper
massacre
lavender
calendar
islander
pillager
villager
manager
voyager
challenger
passenger
messenger
scavenger
publisher
polisher
punisher
nourisher
Britisher
copier
connoisseur
amateur

urtch
(ŭrch)

1

birch
church

lurch
perch
search
smirch

urd (ŭrd)

1

bird
(Byrd)
(burred)
heard
(herd)
curd
blurred
slurred
stirred
third
word
(whirred)

2

songbird
blackbird
snowbird
bluebird
lovebird
inferred
conferred
unheard
recurred
occurred
absurd
reword
seaward
homeward
onward
upward
foreword
(forward)
backward

3

mockingbird
hummingbird
Ladybird
overheard

afterward
(afterword)

urge (ŭrj)

1

urge
scourge
splurge
merge
purge
surge
verge

2

submerge
emerge
diverge
converge

urk (ŭrk)

1

jerk
Kirk
lurk
clerk
smirk
perk
Turk
work
quirk

url (ŭrl)

1

earl
furl
girl
hurl
curl
pearl
(purl)
swirl
whirl

urled
(ŭrld)

1

furled
curled
swirled
world
(whirled)
twirled
burled
hurled

urm (ŭrm)

1

germ
term
worm
squirm
firm
perm

urn (ŭrn)

1

urn
(earn)
burn
churn
fern
learn
spurn
turn
stern
yearn

2

sunburn
heartburn
adjourn
concern
Lucerne
Saturn
return
nocturne
intern
astern

eastern
western
southern
northern

**urned
(ŭrnd)**

1
earned
burned
learned

2
sunburned
adjourned
concerned

urce (ŭrs)

1
hearse
curse
nurse
purse
terse
verse
worse

2
disburse
rehearse
immerse
disperse
adverse
traverse
reverse
diverse
inverse
converse

urst (ŭrst)

1
first
thirst
worst
burst

cursed
Hearst
pursed

2
rehearsed
immersed
traversed
conversed

urt (ŭrt)

1
Bert
dirt
hurt
blurt
flirt
pert
spurt

2
unhurt
alert
inert
expert
assert
concert
exert
insert
avert
subvert
revert
convert
overt
pervert
dessert

3
undershirt
introvert
extrovert

urth (ŭrth)

1
earth
birth

(berth)
mirth
Perth
worth

urv (ŭrv)

1
curve
nerve
serve
swerve

2
unnerve
subserve
deserve
reserve
preserve
conserve

**urved
(ŭrvd)**

1
curved
served

2
unnerved
reserved
preserved
conserved

us (ŭs)

1
us
bus
fuss
plus
thus
muss
pus
cuss

2
discuss
surplus

3
omnibus
dubious
tedious
hideous
nucleus
courteous
envious
marvelous
frivolous
platypus
octopus
barbarous
dangerous
humorous
(humerus)
prosperous
sumptuous
mischievous

ush (ŭsh)

1
hush
lush
blush
flush
plush
slush
mush
crush
thrush

ust (ŭst)

1
bust
(bussed)
fussed
just
lust
rust
thrust
cussed
trust
(trussed)

2

combust
robust
gold dust
stardust
august
unjust
disgust
(discussed)
entrust
distrust
mistrust

ut (ŭt)

1

but
(butt)

gut
hut
cut
mutt
nut
rut
shut
what

2

rebut
uncut
haircut
clear-cut
crosscut
peanut
chestnut
walnut

doughnut
beechnut
somewhat

3

scuttlebutt
hazelnut
butternut
coconut

uv (ŭv)

1

dove
love
glove
shove

2

above
true love

uvved (ŭvd)

1

loved
shoved

uz (ŭz)

1

fuzz
does
buzz
'cuz
was

Double uh (ŭ) sounds

Take in some air and get your lips puckered,
Before you find you're simply too tuckered.

—*"Come Blow Your Horn," lyric by Sammy Cahn,*
music by Jimmy Van Heusen

ubber
(ŭb′ər)

2
blubber
rubber

ubby (ŭb′ē)

2
chubby
hubby
clubby
nubby
scrubby
grubby
tubby
stubby

ubble
(ŭb′əl)

2
double
nubble
bubble
rubble
trouble
stubble

ubbled
(ŭb′əld)

2
doubled
troubled
stubbled

ubbling
(ŭb′lĭng)

2
doubling
troubling
bubbling

uffer (ŭf′ər)

2
duffer
scuffer
bluffer
suffer
fluffer
cuffer
snuffer
huffer
puffer
rougher

uggle
(ŭg′əl)

2
juggle
smuggle
snuggle
struggle

uggler
(ŭg′lər)

2
juggler
smuggler
snuggler
struggler

udges
(ŭj′ĭz)

2
judges
smudges
grudges
nudges
budges

udging
(ŭj′ĭng)

2
fudging
judging
smudging
budging
grudging

3
misjudging
begrudging

uhjun
(ŭj′ən)

2
dudgeon
bludgeon

ukker
(ŭk′ər)

2
pucker
trucker
tucker
mucker
sucker

155

ukking
(ŭk′ĭng)

2
ducking
clucking
plucking
trucking
tucking

ukshun
(ŭk′shən)

3
abduction
deduction
reduction
seduction
production
obstruction
destruction
construction

ukted
(ŭk′tĭd)

3
abducted
deducted
obstructed
instructed
constructed

ukter
(ŭk′tər)

3
conductor
obstructer
instructor

uktiv
(ŭk′tĭv)

3
deductive
seductive

conductive
productive
destructive
instructive
constructive

ulted
(ŭl′tĭd)

3
insulted
consulted
resulted
exulted

umber
(ŭm′bər)

2
lumber
slumber
number
umber
cumber

umble
(ŭm′bəl)

2
bumble
humble
jumble
rumble
crumble
grumble
tumble
stumble
fumble

umbler
(ŭm′blər)

2
fumbler
mumbler

grumbler
stumbler

umbling
(ŭm′blĭng)

2
fumbling
jumbling
mumbling
grumbling
crumbling
stumbling

ummer
(ŭm′ər)

2
summer
hummer
number
plumber

ummy
(ŭm′ē)

2
chummy
dummy
mummy
crummy
tummy
yummy

umming
(ŭm′ĭng)

2
chumming
humming
coming
plumbing
numbing
strumming
thumbing
slumming

umper
(ŭm′pər)

2
bumper
jumper
plumper
pumper
stumper
thumper

umpy
(ŭm′pē)

2
jumpy
slumpy
grumpy

umping
(ŭm′pĭng)

2
bumping
dumping
jumping
lumping
clumping
slumping
pumping
thumping

unching
(ŭn′chĭng)

2
lunching
munching
punching
crunching
bunching

under
(ŭn′dər)

2
under
plunder

thunder
wonder
sunder

**unger
(ŭng′ər)**

2

younger
hunger

unny (ŭn′ē)

2

funny
money
sunny
(sonny)
honey
bunny

**unning
(ŭn′ĭng)**

2

running
sunning
stunning
dunning
punning

**unky
(ŭng′kē)**

2

funky
junky
flunky
punky

**upper
(ŭp′ər)**

2

upper
scupper
supper

**urches
(ŭr′chĭz)**

2

churches
birches
perches
searches
lurches

**urging
(ŭr′jĭng)**

2

splurging
scourging
urging
merging
purging

3

submerging
emerging
immerging
converging

**urking
(ŭr′kĭng)**

2

jerking
smirking
perking
working
irking
lurking

**urmer
(ŭr′mər)**

2

firmer
murmur
wormer

**urning
(ŭr′nĭng)**

2

earning
spurning
burning
churning
learning
turning
yearning

3

discerning
concerning
returning

**urnish
(ŭr′nĭsh)**

2

burnish
furnish

**ursez
(ŭr′sĭz)**

3

rehearses
submerses
immerses
traverses
reverses

**ursing
(ŭr′sĭng)**

2

cursing
nursing

3

coercing
rehearsing
immersing

**ursive
(ŭr′sĭv)**

3

coercive
perversive

**urted
(ŭr′tĭd)**

2

skirted
flirted
squirted
spurted

3

asserted
inserted
concerted
reverted

**urtin
(ŭrt′n)**

2

curtain
certain

**urting
(ŭr′tĭng)**

2

hurting
skirting
shirting
spurting
squirting
flirting

3

alerting
exerting
inserting
reverting

urtle
(ŭr′təl)

2 ——————

myrtle
fertile
turtle

urvent
(ŭr′vənt)

2 ——————

fervent
servant

urving
(ŭr′vĭng)

2 ——————

Irving
curving
serving
swerving

urvless
(ŭrv′lĭs)

2 ——————

nerveless
swerveless

urzhun
(ŭr′zhən)

3 ——————

excursion
immersion
subversion
diversion
submersion

usher
(ŭsh′ər)

2 ——————

gusher
usher
plusher
flusher

rusher
crusher
brusher

ushing
(ŭsh′ĭng)

2 ——————

gushing
flushing
brushing
crushing

ushun
(ŭsh′ən)

3 ——————

percussion
concussion
discussion

ussel
(ŭs′əl)

2 ——————

hustle
muscle
tussle
bustle
rustle

ussler
(ŭs′lər)

2 ——————

hustler
rustler

usted
(ŭs′tid)

2 ——————

busted
dusted

rusted
crusted
trusted
lusted

uster
(ŭs′tər)

2 ——————

duster
luster
bluster
fluster
cluster
muster

usterd
(ŭs′tərd)

2 ——————

custard
blustered
mustard
(mustered)
clustered

ustful
(ŭst′fəl)

2 ——————

lustful
trustful

usty
(ŭs′tē)

2 ——————

busty
dusty
rusty
crusty
musty
trusty

usting
(ŭs′tĭng)

2 ——————

busting
dusting
trusting

utter (ŭt′ər)

2 ——————

butter
flutter
sputter
shutter
mutter
utter
gutter
cutter

utton
(ŭt′ən)

2 ——————

button
mutton
glutton

uvver
(ŭv′ər)

2 ——————

lover
shover
glover
hover

uvving
(ŭv′ĭng)

2 ——————

loving
shoving

uzzen
(ŭz′ən)

uzzle
(ŭz′əl)

2
dozen
cousin

2
muzzle
nuzzle
puzzle
guzzle

How to Sell, Copyright, and Publish a Song

Any aspiring songwriter who is serious about his or her work should develop an equally serious interest in the legal, business, and copyright aspects of songwriting. Essentially, being a songwriter eventually involves affiliation with one or more of the performing-rights organizations who not only act as agents between songwriters and song publishers but who also license the right to perform members' songs on the radio or television, in concert, etc.

Further information about the customary terms of membership in these organizations and about their activities on behalf of their members can be obtained by writing any or all of the following:

ASCAP
American Society of Composers,
    Authors & Publishers
1 Lincoln Plaza
New York, N.Y. 10023

(ask for their helpful pamphlet,
    "How to Get Your Song Published")

BMI
Broadcast Music Inc.
320 West 57th St.
New York, N.Y. 10019

SESAC Inc.
10 Columbus Circle
New York, N.Y. 10019

The American Guild of Authors and Composers (AGAC) represents *only* songwriters (i.e., not publishers as well) and describes itself as "a voluntary national songwriters' association run by and for songwriters." Its role is to help songwriters in matters of contracts and royalty collection. More information can be obtained by writing:

AGAC
American Guild of Authors & Composers
40 West 57th St.
New York, N.Y. 10019

(Membership in AGAC presupposes membership in one of the other organizations mentioned above.)

160